THEY LIKE JESUS
BUT NOT THE CHURCH
Participant's Guide

Books by Dan Kimball

The Emerging Church

Emerging Worship

Listening to the Beliefs of Emerging Churches (contributor)

They Like Jesus but Not the Church

Do You Like Jesus but Not the Church? (forthcoming)

THEY LIKE JESUS BUT NOT THE CHURCH

Participant's Guide

Six Sessions Responding to Culture's Objections to Christianity

DAN KIMBALL

with Margaret Feinberg

ZONDERVAN®

ZONDERVAN.com/
AUTHORTRACKER
follow your favorite authors

They Like Jesus but Not the Church Participant's Guide
Copyright © 2008 by Dan Kimball

Requests for information should be addressed to:

Zondervan, *Grand Rapids, Michigan 49530*

ISBN 978-0-310-27794-1

All Scripture quotations, unless otherwise indicated, are taken from the *Holy Bible, New International Version®*. NIV®. Copyright © 1973, 1978, 1984 by International Bible Society. Used by permission of Zondervan. All rights reserved.

Scripture quotations marked TNIV are taken from the *Holy Bible, Today's New International Version™*. TNIV®. Copyright © 2001, 2005 by International Bible Society. Used by permission of Zondervan. All rights reserved.

Internet addresses (websites, blogs, etc.) and telephone numbers printed in this book are offered as a resource to you. These are not intended in any way to be or imply an endorsement on the part of Zondervan, nor do we vouch for the content of these sites and numbers for the life of this book.

Interior design adapted by Beth Shagene

Printed in the United States of America

09 10 11 12 13 14 • 25 24 23 22 21 20 19 18 17 16 15 14 13 12 11 10 9 8 7 6 5 4

CONTENTS

INTRODUCTION

In a time of increasingly depressing national statistics about how many people are disconnecting from church and how culture is negatively thinking of Christians, I have a lot of hope and optimism. The reason is because even though people may have negative experiences with the church and Christianity, they respect Jesus and are usually quite interested in him.

It is a paradox very much like what Mahatma Gandhi once expressed when he said:

"I like your Christ. I do not like your Christians. They are so unlike your Christ."

What an incredibly crazy thing to hear: that people like Jesus, but not the church or Christians. Why are Jesus' followers giving off such negative impressions? Are there valid reasons that people feel this way? Are their negative perceptions about the gospel itself or about how the gospel is presented and lived out? How do we respond to these perceptions?

JESUS CARES ABOUT THOSE OUTSIDE THE CHURCH — SO WHY WOULDN'T WE?

I am personally thrilled that you are studying *They Like Jesus but Not the Church*, because it's quite tempting to simply ignore what people outside the church think. We could just go along in life, busy with our jobs, families, friends, and church activities — slowly but surely losing our passion to care for those outside the church. But choosing to participate in this study shows that you care about those Jesus cared about. Jesus spent time with known "sinners" (Matt. 9:10 – 13). He died and sacrificed his life for sinners (Rom. 5:8). And he sent out his disciples — that includes you and me — to be salt and light to fellow sinners (Matt. 5:13 – 16; Acts 1:8).

7

But being salt and light means taking the time to place ourselves in situations and relationships with people outside the church; it means listening to them and trying to understand them. But many of us aren't stopping to listen. We like doing all the talking. Now, more than ever, it is important to *hear* our culture's questions in order to give meaningful answers. After all, in the Scriptures is the well-known passage:

> Always be prepared to give an answer to everyone who *asks you* to give the reason for the hope that you have. But do this with gentleness and respect, keeping a clear conscience, so that those who speak maliciously against your good behavior in Christ may be ashamed of their slander.
>
> *1 PETER 3:15–16 (EMPHASIS ADDED)*

The reality is that for people to be able to ask us, we must be listening and in a place of trust. Trust comes through time and relationship. In these sessions you will hear the perceptions and questions about Christianity and the church from some friends of mine with whom I have done my best to build trust.

TAKING TIME TO HEAR THE HEART OF THOSE ALL AROUND US

During this study, you may become uncomfortable hearing some of these questions and impressions people have of the church and Christians today. Some questions may even make you defensive. But as you will see in the DVD, these are real people with real lives, not just statistics to simply be glanced over or dismissed. When you look into their eyes, listen to their stories, and hear their hearts, perhaps you will begin to understand why they feel the way they do. Besides, you will likely hear in their questions and perceptions the very questions and perceptions of people all around you in your community, workplace, school, or even in your family. In this study we will explore and wrestle with ways to respond biblically to these questions and perceptions.

PLEASE PRAY AS YOU GO THROUGH THESE SESSIONS

There is something very important to remember as we proceed. We can listen to those who like Jesus but not the church and even address their concerns. But the fact is that it will be the Spirit of God who will move in someone's life to open his or her heart and mind to who Jesus really is. It is the gospel that is alive and active and will powerfully change an individual, not our apologetics or profound answers (Rom. 1:16). It is the cross of Jesus and his Spirit where the power comes from. God *uses* what we say and do, but it is God who changes people. One way that God uses us is to build trust with people, so they will listen. Unfortunately, many of those who like Jesus but not the church aren't listening because they don't trust many of the Christian voices they hear. That's why we need to be faithfully praying for these people *and* faithfully praying as we think through and discuss ways of addressing their perceptions of the church and Christianity.

My prayer is that, as we talk to people about Jesus, they will come to a full understanding of who the Jesus of the Bible truly is. Often they know he is a man of peace and love, but don't know that he is also Savior. Often they see him as a Martin Luther King Jr. or Gandhi type leader, but don't yet understand that he was not merely a human being, but divine. They may believe Jesus taught us to care for our neighbor and the oppressed, but often don't know that Jesus took on our sin and will one day come back in judgment. People need to know the biblical Jesus and the full life and eternal life that putting faith in him brings. And when they come to know the Jesus of the Bible, they will more readily accept the fact that the church is part of Jesus' plan. The church is Jesus' bride that he loves despite its faults. You can't like Jesus, but not like his bride.

May God use these sessions in your life, and may you have an optimistic, depressing, difficult, joyful, uncomfortable, and hopeful time as you explore the challenges that will be asked for the sake of the gospel and for the sake of the lives of those who like Jesus but not the church.

DAN KIMBALL

www.dankimball.com
www.theylikejesus.com

9

HOW TO USE THIS STUDY

They Like Jesus but Not the Church is a DVD curriculum for those interested in being able to respond to the challenging questions asked about Christianity and the church today. This curriculum is based on the book of the same name that was written and designed for church leaders. For more information about that book, please visit *www.theylikejesus.com*.

Each session begins with a DVD introduction in which Dan Kimball shares opening thoughts and insights on the given topic, then interviews someone about his or her own experiences. Once you finish watching the first video segment, you'll choose from a series of questions to discuss.

Then you'll move on to the second video segment in which Dan talks in greater depth about the subject, followed by more questions to reflect on and discuss. Both group discussions include pertinent Scripture passages to interact with, so you'll want to keep your Bible nearby.

Some of the questions asked might be difficult to answer on your own. In the appendix, we have provided answers to the more theological questions to help guide you in responding to those. You will see by the questions which ones have answers in the appendix.

Finally, you'll have the opportunity to put what you have studied into practice by selecting at least one activity from the "How You Can Respond" section. Share your experiences with the group during the following session.

Please begin and/or end each session with prayer. As important as it is to talk and read about how to respond to the culture's questions about Christianity and the church—and do our part—we must never forget that it is only God who can change hearts and lives. So please take prayer seriously as you study together.

Also, whether you are doing this study with a group of friends or in a class, we encourage you to be constantly thinking about how to share what you are learning with others. The topics explored are designed to be talked about with all kinds of people—hopefully some of whom you haven't even met yet.

THE DANGER OF THE CHRISTIAN BUBBLE

In J.R.R. Tolkien's *The Fellowship of the Ring,* Galadriel, the elf queen played by Kate Blanchett in the movie, says a classic line about the changes happening in Middle Earth. She says to Frodo, "The world is changed. I feel it in the water. I feel it in the earth. I smell it in the air."

THEY LIKE JESUS BUT NOT THE CHURCH, P. 15

DVD SEGMENT #1

Let's watch as Dan Kimball talks to various students at a local college campus about their impressions of Jesus and then discusses their responses. With each video clip throughout the study, space for note-taking is provided here in the participant's guide.

DVD Notes
Students' impressions of Jesus

Students' impressions of Christians

The four phases of being a Christian

Phase 1: We become Christians

Phase 2: We become part of church life

Phase 3: We enter the Christian bubble

Phase 4: We become Jonah Christians

The Christian bubble

GROUP STUDY AND DISCUSSION #1

1. If you were to ask the same questions from the DVD presentation at a local college campus in your community, do you think you would hear similar answers or different ones? Explain.

2. Why is it is so easy to be in the Christian bubble? Are there benefits of being in the bubble?

3. Do you think you could possibly be in the bubble yourself or headed that direction? Identify ways you may be in the bubble or approaching it.

4. Look up the following Scriptures. What does each reveal about what it means to be living outside of the bubble and escaping the bubble if you need to?

Matthew 5:13–16

Matthew 28:16–20

John 17:15–18

EXTRA: What do you think Jesus meant in this passage by "the world"? What do you think he meant by "evil"? *(See appendix, pages 107–108, for responses.)*

Acts 1:7–8

EXTRA: In this passage, what was the primary reason Jesus said the Holy Spirit was going to be sent?

5. Jesus said we are to be salt and light to our culture, but Scripture also tells us to support and care for the community of believers. How do we balance both of these roles in our week-to-week lives?

DVD SEGMENT #2

Let's watch as Dan Kimball talks about how even the pop culture versions of Jesus can become a launching point to talking about issues of faith.

> IF YOU STAY IN THE BUBBLE LONG ENOUGH, YOU BEGIN TO PRODUCE WEIRD THINGS.
> —FROM THE DVD

DVD Notes
Jesus bobblehead and Pink Jesus

Starting point for a conversation about Jesus

Two friends

Rumors and misperceptions of Christians in the early church

The pop-culture version of Jesus

GROUP STUDY AND DISCUSSION #2

1. What do you think Jesus would say about being made into a bobblehead?

2. Why do you think people are so fascinated with Jesus?

3. How would *you* describe the biblical Jesus? What may be the difference between the pop-culture version of Jesus and the biblical Jesus? What are key things about the biblical Jesus that everyone should know? *(See appendix, pages 108 – 110, for responses.)*

EXTRA: As trust is built in any relationship with a non-Christian, the need to articulate the gospel will eventually arise. Can you define "the gospel"? What Bible passages would you turn to? *(See appendix, page 110, for suggested responses.)*

Dan describes a gap between people and God created by sin as well as a prior gap that exists because of people's misconceptions of Christianity.

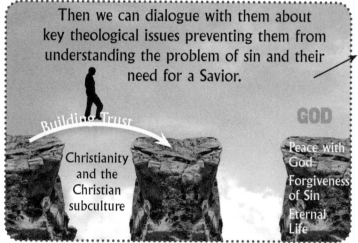

Then we can dialogue with them about key theological issues preventing them from understanding the problem of sin and their need for a Savior.

Building Trust

Christianity and the Christian subculture

GOD

Peace with God
Forgiveness of Sin
Eternal Life

Judgmentalism

Religious pluralism

Scripture

Salvation

Jesus

Right now, because of the chasm of Christianity and the Christian subculture, many never get to this point.

Building Trust

Christianity and the Christian subculture

GOD

SIN

Peace with God
Forgiveness of Sin
Eternal Life

4. Review the diagrams on pages 20 and 21. In what ways have you found the message of these diagrams to be true? Do you think people today stumble more over the gospel or their perceptions of Christianity and the church?

5. Read John 17:14. Some Christians may argue, "Of course we will be hated—Jesus predicted that." Do you think Christians today are hated for the gospel message or for the way they're delivering it (their attitude and approach to talking about Jesus and salvation)?

6. In what ways is it a cop-out to use the "they will hate you because you're a Christian" argument to justify that, of course, people won't like Christians and the church?

7. Read Matthew 9:9–13 and 9:35–37. In the first passage, Jesus is criticized by the Pharisees for eating with sinners. In the second passage, we are told how Jesus had compassion for people. The word *compassion* means to "have the bowels yearn," expressing a pain deep within. In other words, Jesus felt extreme anguish over the people who were without a spiritual shepherd.

When you think of people who do not know Jesus, do you ever experience that kind of compassion or anguish?

What stops you from aching over people who have never met Jesus?

Why are trust and relationship so important when talking to people in today's culture about Jesus and Christianity?

WRAP-UP

Pray that while we exist in biblical Christian community, we do not become isolated and removed from the very people with whom Jesus wants us to be in relationships, so we can share Jesus with them. Pray, as Jesus prayed for his disciples in John 17:15, that we not be taken from the world but protected from it evils.

> May we move
> from living as citizens
> of the bubble to

> Living as
> missional citizens
> of the kingdom

HOW YOU CAN RESPOND

Choose at least one of the following suggested activities/reflections to complete over the next week. Consider sharing with your friends or small group members the impact the activity or reflection has on you.

1. Who are you specifically praying for right now that is not a Christian? Write down the names of two people who do not know Jesus. Pray for them daily throughout the remaining weeks of this study.

   Name: _____

   Name: _____

2. When was the last time you went out with someone who is not a Christian—to a movie, dinner, or just to hang out? Share what it was like. If you haven't recently socialized with a non-Christian, what are your reasons?

Make a commitment to spend time with at least one person who is not a Christian during the remaining weeks of this study. And, if it feels like it wouldn't be awkward, ask that person a question or two about what you are discussing in this study. A great and easy way to have a conversation with someone is to ask what he or she thinks of Jesus, and then what he or she thinks of the church and Christianity. These are fairly nonthreatening questions that usually result in lively responses. Don't feel the need to counter what the person may say. Just listen. If the opportunity arises, consider even asking his or her perceptions of other topics this study addresses. Confidentially share your experiences with your group.

3. If you find you are living inside the Christian bubble, make a list of things you can intentionally do to break out of the bubble.

Consider ways that you could intentionally meet others outside of the church world. It doesn't mean that you walk up to strangers and start talking to them. Perhaps there is a coworker (or neighbor or classmate) whom you have never bothered getting to know better. Think of people who may share similar interests (music, sports, hobbies), so friendships can more naturally be established. Think of parents with children in the same life stage as yours who you may be able to connect with at school events. It takes time — but if you are praying and thinking strategically, there are ways to meet people and naturally connect with them. Over time and as trust is built, you may find the opportunity to ask questions about what they may think of church or Christians — as they discover you are one — or about their personal beliefs. Don't feel as if you awkwardly have to force a conversation about Jesus.

If you are praying, God will show you when it's appropriate to ask questions. The key is building trust. Trust takes time, but people are worth it. In the meantime you are sharing life with them and caring for them as Jesus would. (See the recommended resources box on the next page for further ideas.)

Write down names of people with whom you aren't friends yet, but with whom you may already have a connection that you could develop into a friendship. Think of any intentional way you could put yourself in new environments or in new circles of people outside the church. And then take at least some initial steps to begin building (or renewing) a friendship over the next five weeks.

RECOMMENDED RESOURCES
FOR FURTHER STUDY

Three very practical books about personally connecting with those outside of the church:

Evangelism without Additives: What If Sharing Your Faith Meant Just Sharing Yourself? by Jim Henderson, WaterBrook, 2005

Just Walk Across the Room by Bill Hybels, Zondervan, 2006

Becoming a Contagious Christian by Bill Hybels and Mark Mittelberg, Zondervan, 1994

If you are interested in examining the broader impact culture has on the church and Christianity as well as the need for missional living, check out:

The Emerging Church: Vintage Christianity for New Generations by Dan Kimball, Zondervan, 2003

Exiles: Living Missionally in a Post-Christian Culture by Mike Frost, Hendrickson, 2006

www.rockrebel.com

www.thunderstruck.org

IS THE CHURCH NEGATIVE, JUDGMENTAL, AND POLITICAL?

> "The church is a group of judgmental mudslingers. They seem to really like picking fights with others. Whether it is homosexuals, or other religions, or even with each other."
>
> *GARY, IN THEY LIKE JESUS BUT NOT THE CHURCH, P. 99*

DVD SEGMENT #1

Let's watch as Dan Kimball explores the idea that Christians are more often known as judgmental and negative people rather than loving and kind people who have discovered God's grace. In this first video clip, Dan will also interview Gary about his experiences.

DVD Notes

A young guy with tattoos and piercings

An apologetic pastor

A Bible of "don'ts"

Gary

Decide what you want to believe

The approach of Christians

GROUP STUDY AND DISCUSSION #1

1. Like the pastor in Dan's story who made a generalized judgment about people with tattoos and piercings, what are other ways Christians often judge others without knowing them? Have you ever done this? Explain.

2. Why do you think Christians have a reputation for being judgmental? Why do you think Christians are more often known for what they're against rather than what they're for?

3. Read Galatians 5:22–23. List the attributes the Spirit produces in us and what we should be known for.

Which of the attributes in Galatians 5:22–23 do you think you may be known for among your non-Christian friends?

Which of the attributes do you want to be known for that maybe you currently aren't?

4. If someone outside the church could hear you talk, would he or she hear you saying more positive or negative things about what it really means to follow Jesus? How about people in your church? How about sermons you listen to?

5. Politics and Christianity is a huge issue, but many feel that Christians use politics and politicians use Christians in negative ways. Do you feel this is true? Where do you see it happening most often?

Would Jesus be Republican, Democrat, or independent? (Obviously, there is no right answer to this question, but have some fun thinking about it.)

DVD SEGMENT #2

Let's watch as Dan Kimball talks about the negative perceptions of Christianity and why our approach to sharing our faith is so important.

DVD Notes

Story of a mother becoming a Buddhist

Should Christians judge other people?

Dan's story of a teenager in his youth group

Judging those outside the church

People who are different than you

Guilt- or grace-driven?

> I DON'T ADVOCATE HOLDING BACK WHEN IT COMES TO
> TALKING ABOUT SIN ... BUT I AM SAYING THAT WE SHOULD
> DO IT AT THE RIGHT TIME WITH THE RIGHT ATTITUDE.
>
> *THEY LIKE JESUS BUT NOT THE CHURCH, P. 110*

GROUP STUDY AND DISCUSSION #2

1. A verse often quoted is Matthew 7:1 in which Jesus instructed, "Do not judge." What do you think Jesus specifically meant here—that no one will be judged or that Christians should not "judge" other people? *(See appendix, pages 111–112, for a response.)*

EXTRA: As the topic of tattoos came up in Dan's and Gary's remarks, are you aware of the Bible verse some Christians use to judge that tattoos are inappropriate? *(See appendix, page 112, for a response.)*

2. You may not judge someone for having tattoos and piercings, as in the DVD example. But do you subtly judge people in other ways? People with different political views or musical tastes? People who wear suits and ties or drive expensive cars? Give some examples.

3. The apostle Paul taught the Corinthian church that there is a difference between judging Christians and judging those outside the church. Read 1 Corinthians 5:12 – 13. Who does it say should judge those outside the church? Who does it say should judge those inside the church? What is the difference between the two? *(See appendix, page 113, for responses.)*

4. Read Galatians 6:1 – 10. What should you do if a fellow Christian is caught in sin? What is the goal of such a response?

5. Read Matthew 18:15–20. What additional things do you learn here about responding to a fellow Christian's sin? What should the church do when a Christian sins?

6. When you reflect on the life of Jesus and his interactions, with whom did he get the most upset? Why?

7. What was the heart of Jesus like toward those who rejected him, as seen in Luke 19:41? How is your heart compared to his about those outside the church?

WRAP-UP

Pray that instead of Christians (and the church) being known as judgmental and critical, we will be known as positive agents of change, loving others as Jesus does. Pray that your non-Christian acquaintances will see Jesus in you.

> May we move from being known as a judgmental, negative people to

> Being known as positive agents of change, loving others as Jesus does, showing the fruit of the Spirit in our lives

HOW YOU CAN RESPOND

Choose at least one of the following suggested activities/reflections to complete over the next week. Consider sharing with your friends or small group members the impact the activity or reflection has on you.

1. Take a few moments to think about your own life. Your words. Your heart and attitude. If people you know outside the church were to describe what they observe in your life, words, and actions about what it means to be a Christian, what would they say? Without even knowing Galatians 5:22–23, do you think someone would describe the fruit of the Spirit when thinking of you?

2. This week be particularly aware of your words and attitudes as you are in your workplace or among those who are not Christians. You may be the only Christian they personally know, and what you do and say as well as your attitudes will make a major difference in how they think of Christians and the church.

3. Spend some time in prayer, asking God to open your eyes to the people in your life you may have been judging without even realizing it. Ask God to reveal his heart on each person and situation. If appropriate, ask the person for forgiveness and grace.

4. Take a few moments to look at your church website and other Christian websites. When people visit the site, what do they see that shows your church as a positive light that influences the world? Is there information about your church's involvement with the poor and those in need? Look at sermon titles and wording. Is your church portrayed more for what it stands or for what it stands against?

5. Evaluate your own life and the life of your church in regard to what you are doing to be a positive light for Jesus in your community as well as globally. What are you doing to help the poor or oppressed? If you aren't taking any action, why not?

RECOMMENDED RESOURCES FOR FURTHER STUDY

Churches That Make a Difference: Reaching Your Community with Good News and Good Works by Ron Sider, Baker, 2002. This book provides examples of individuals and churches that break stereotypes and are positive influences in their communities through social justice projects and services.

Honest to God? Becoming an Authentic Christian by Bill Hybels, Zondervan, 1992. This book asks the question of whether or not we are living lives that are truly salt and light and discusses the importance of living with integrity.

In the Name of Jesus by Henri Nouwen, Crossroad, 1993. A book that shows the importance of living a life modeled after Jesus.

The Irresistible Revolution: Living as an Ordinary Radical by Shane Claiborne, Zondervan, 2006. The compelling adventure of someone who takes very seriously Jesus' words to care for the needy and oppressed.

DOES THE CHURCH RESTRICT AND OPPRESS WOMEN?

"I feel that the church is very sexist, yet I don't believe that Jesus was sexist. From what I have observed, women in the church basically sit on the sidelines and are only able to work with children, answer the phones, be secretaries, and serve the men. They seem to be given no voice. The church seems pretty much like a boys' club for adults."

ALICIA, IN THEY LIKE JESUS BUT NOT THE CHURCH, P. 115

DVD SEGMENT #1

In the first video clip for session three, let's watch as Dan Kimball begins to explore why many see the church as male-dominated and female-oppressing. He then follows up by interviewing a woman named Erika about her experiences.

DVD Notes
1950s diner

Image of what a family is supposed to be

What men and women were supposed to be

Boys' club for adults

Erika

Equal footing

Jesus — the first to question the status quo

GROUP STUDY AND DISCUSSION #1

1. Why do you think some would describe the church as a "boys' club for adults"?

Have you or someone you know been hurt by the "boys' club" mentality in the workplace or anywhere in general in our culture today? What about in the church? Describe the experience and the aftereffect.

2. What would Erika experience or encounter if she came to your church? Would she hear any subtle jokes or innuendoes about the roles of women? What, if anything, do you think it would take to make Erika feel comfortable and welcome in your church while staying within your theological beliefs?

3. Dan tells the story of a church leader who said, "She's just a secretary; why would I ask her?" It wasn't meant to be a harmful comment, but what does this communicate about the woman's value as a person and her contribution to the direction of the church? What does it say about her value as an employee? As a child of God? Have you ever heard Christians make comments like this?

4. Do you think gender issues are becoming more or less important to this generation than previous generations? Explain.

DVD SEGMENT #2

Let's watch as Dan Kimball discusses the perceptions of women in the church and why our attitude toward this issue is so important.

DVD Notes
The importance of integrating women into the church

Two views

Complementarian

Egalitarian

Breaking taboos

Women and the church

GROUP STUDY AND DISCUSSION #2

Over the centuries, the church has had differences of opinions on the role of women in the church. Even today, godly Christians study this issue and come to alternate conclusions. Depending on your church, you may or may not have women in leadership roles, such as pastor or elder. Some of these questions may or may not apply to you.

The focus of this session is neither to debate differing views of women in ministry nor to offer a full study on the theology of women in church leadership. Instead, we will highlight the importance of recognizing and respecting each theological viewpoint, with the goal of helping you use the lens of Scripture to understand what you believe and why you believe it. This is an extremely significant issue in our emerging culture that we must be ready to address intelligently and lovingly, no matter what our personal beliefs.

The two primary viewpoints of women in church leadership (and there are various degrees within each in actual practice) are the following:

COMPLEMENTARIAN: The viewpoint that women can serve in many ways in the church, but that leadership roles, such as elder, pastor, or primary teacher, are restricted to men.

EGALITARIAN: The viewpoint that women can serve in any leadership role of the church including pastor, primary teacher, or elder.

AS A CHURCH, ARE WE REFLECTING THE WHOLENESS OF GOD AND THE FACT THAT HUMAN BEINGS, BOTH MALES AND FEMALES, ARE CREATED IN GOD'S IMAGE?
THEY LIKE JESUS BUT NOT THE CHURCH, P. 121

1. Which viewpoint does your church hold?

2. Which of the viewpoints have you really studied in depth? What can you learn from studying both?

3. Read 1 Corinthians 14:34–35 and 1 Timothy 2:11–15 aloud and then discuss how you would explain these passages. Imagine looking a twenty-five-year-old, well-educated female in the eyes as you read them. *(See appendix, pages 115–119, for suggested responses.)*

4. Imagine another scenario: You are serving as one of the leaders in the high school ministry at your church, and a ninth-grade girl becomes a Christian through the youth group. Her parents contact you. Though they are not Christians, they have heard good things about your church. But they also have a few concerns. They have read some Bible verses that sound strange (the two passages from question 3) and are afraid their daughter will be influenced in regard to her worth and potential. How would you answer their questions about whether their daughter will really have to remain silent and never teach or speak in church? How would you respond to their questioning the Scripture that says their daughter isn't saved until she bears a child?

5. Imagine that a godly, Spirit-filled Christian male and a godly, Spirit-filled Christian female are each given the same Bible, commentaries, and word study tools and sent off to different rooms to study the same chapter of the Bible. After several hours of prayer and study, each produces a teaching outline that is exactly the same. Can both enter a pulpit and preach a sermon based on their notes to a mixed-gender audience? Why or why not? Now what if the setting wasn't a pulpit but a Christian education classroom?

6. Read the following summary by Dan Kimball and then list some specific examples of how Jesus valued women.

> While the cultural norm for a rabbi or Jewish leader would have been to *not* include females when he was teaching, Jesus did the opposite. Jesus was once invited into a home of two sisters, Mary and Martha. Mary was sitting at his feet in the posture of a rabbi's disciple, a place generally reserved for men. When Martha asked her sister to help her in the kitchen, Jesus basically told Martha to get out of the kitchen and listen to his teaching instead.
>
> As Jesus traveled, he was not only accompanied by male followers but also female followers. For these women to travel with the group would have been viewed as scandalous. Ironically, the females in this traveling group were the ones who supplied the financial needs of Jesus and the disciples.
>
> Not only did Jesus break the rabbinic laws of his time by teaching and talking to women, but he went even further. He allowed women to touch him, even women who were considered "unclean." Jesus touched a dead woman, the daughter of a synagogue ruler, and brought her back to life. He also allowed a woman who was known as a "sinner" to wash his feet while he was dining at the home of a disapproving religious leader. It is unknown what the woman's sin was—but some speculate it may have been prostitution, which would have been all the more reason for Jesus to avoid her touch, according to the religious laws and customs of the day.
>
> Interestingly, the very first people Jesus chose to appear to after he rose from the dead were women.

7. While still respecting its theological position on this issue, are there any ways in which your church is missing the opportunity to integrate women into ministry? Discuss some possibilities.

WRAP-UP

Pray that instead of the church and Christians being known as dominated by males and oppressing women, we will be known as those who hold women in the highest respect and include them in the leadership of the church in the highest regard our church theologically allows.

May we move from being known as those who restrict and oppress women to

Being known as those who honor and revere women and help them lead the church in the areas of their giftedness

HOW YOU CAN RESPOND

Choose at least one of the following suggested activities/reflections to complete over the next week. Consider sharing with your friends or small group members the impact the activity or reflection has on you.

1. No matter what your viewpoint on women's leadership roles in the church, can you articulately, intelligently, and lovingly respond to the controversial passages mentioned in this sesson? If not, you may need to do some further homework to be able to adequately answer someone in our culture today who asks why you believe as you do.

2. Is there anything in your attitude and heart you need to confess or deal with in regard to those who have a different viewpoint on this issue than you do?

3. Is there anything in your attitude toward women which may be subtly negative or demeaning?

RECOMMENDED RESOURCES
FOR FURTHER STUDY

Two Views on Women in Ministry edited by Craig Blomberg, Zondervan, 2005. This book is an incredible resource because it's written by theologians who discuss each of the viewpoints of women in ministry. The arguments on both sides are strong and thoughtful and will help you understand a different perspective as well as strengthen your own.

Men and Women in the Church: Building Consensus on Christian Leadership by Sara Sumner, InterVarsity Press, 2003. The author shares her own journey as a woman in the church while drawing on scholarly discussion of the issue.

www.cbeinternational.org—The website of Christians for Biblical Equality, which supports the egalitarian perspective.

www.cbmw.org—The website of the Council for Biblical Manhood and Womanhood, which supports the complementarian perspective.

IS THE CHURCH HOMOPHOBIC?

"When I was volunteering at the gay center, I would be on the phone talking to teenagers in trouble and feeling I was making a positive difference in the world. But then I'd go out to my car and find tracts which would utterly condemn me left by Christians on my car windshield. I'd look at these heartless words with little pieces of Bible verses quoted out of context and wonder, Why do they hate me so much? Why don't they even have the decency to come in and talk to me rather than leave anger and hate on my windshield and run?"

PENNY, IN THEY LIKE JESUS BUT NOT THE CHURCH, P. 141

DVD SEGMENT #1

Let's watch as Dan Kimball discusses the perceptions of how the church and Christians are responding to the issue of homosexuality and interviews Penny on the topic.

DVD Notes

Hair salon story

A cultural openness to homosexuality

Words that were used to describe homosexuals

The picture the church is painting

Penny

Ranch experience

Pain

GROUP STUDY AND DISCUSSION #1

This is a controversial issue and, again, one about which we don't have time for deep theological study. Dan Kimball personally takes a conservative theological position in regard to the practice of homosexuality. You may have a differing viewpoint. Regardless of your perspective, please consider the following questions and Scripture study as a way of helping those who feel the church is homophobic to realize that such an attitude is not the norm for most churches.

1. Why do you think some Christians approach the issue of homosexuality with some fear and even anger?

Have you personally seen poor examples of how the church has treated homosexuals? Have you personally seen positive examples? Explain.

2. As you listened to Penny's story, what struck you most? Did the comments of the Christian ranch hand surprise you, or have you heard comments like this before?

3. Penny says, "My defense mechanisms toward Christians began to rise pretty quick." Why do you think that happened? What kinds of statements, attitudes, and activities can make people's defense mechanisms rise as we're building relationships with them?

4. Imagine that an unmarried couple who are living together and are sexually active enter your church. They sit, one with an arm around the other, appropriately expressing affection. You meet them after the service. They tell you that they aren't Christians yet, but are interested in God and checking out your church further. Now imagine the couple is gay.

How would your reactions differ? How would your church respond?

Theologically, what is the difference been the straight couple and the homosexual couple? How are the two couples different in Jesus' eyes?

DVD SEGMENT #2

Let's watch as Dan Kimball talks about developing a healthy response to the issue of homosexuality from a biblical perspective.

DVD Notes
Story of Karen

Knowing what the Bible says about homosexuality

Recognizing different arguments

The power of friendship

Thinking about the issue

GROUP STUDY AND DISCUSSION #2

1. Do you feel that your church is a safe place for people struggling with same-sex attraction? What would they hear from the pulpit?

2. How does portraying homosexuality as "sinister" and "wrong" make those struggling with same-sex attraction feel uncomfortable talking about it?

3. There is a fast-rising tide of pro-gay theological interpretations of the Bible. These arguments are especially popular at universities and on the Internet and are acknowledged and becoming more commonly accepted by both straight and gay people.

   Even if we believe that the Bible says the practice of homosexuality is considered sin, we cannot simply ignore the counterarguments out there. Knowing the key theological arguments regarding homosexuality is extremely important in conversing with our culture today.

   Reflect on the following arguments (pages 60–65) and how you would explain each one. Interpretations from a pro-gay theological viewpoint are provided here. *(Interpretations from a conservative viewpoint are found in the appendix, pages 121 – 127.)*

The Sin of Sodom — Genesis 19

We generally have taught that the primary sin of Sodom in Genesis 19 was homosexuality. Yet neither Jesus nor any of the five prophets who mention Sodom talk about the sexual sin that led to Sodom's destruction. Ezekiel 16:49 says that the sin of Sodom was its lack of hospitality and not helping the poor — not homosexuality. Another argument is that the sin of Sodom was gang rape, not consensual homosexual sex.

How do you respond to these claims that the church has misused Sodom and labeled its destruction as judgment for homosexuality, when the Scriptures themselves say it was about lack of hospitality and neglecting the poor and needy?

Leviticus Passages — Leviticus 18:22 and 20:13

Featured in tracts, on signs, and quoted in sermons, Leviticus 18:22 and 20:13 are the most popular verses Christians have used when presenting a "case closed, no more questions" response to the issue of homosexuality.

Yet there are growing questions about how these isolated verses have been used for such a defense. For example, if Christians use these verses to say homosexuality is a sin, then why don't they also obey other verses from Leviticus? Leviticus 19:19 says to not wear fabrics woven of two different kinds of material. Leviticus 19:27 says not to cut the hair at the sides of your head or off the edges of your beard. Leviticus 20:9 says if a child curses his mother or father he is to be killed. Leviticus 20:10 says if a man and woman commit adultery they are to be killed. Leviticus 11:7–8 says we shouldn't touch a dead pig. (And backing up, Exodus 21:7 says it's okay to sell your daughter as a slave, while Exodus 35:2 says to kill someone if they work on the Sabbath.) Obviously, most Christians today don't hold to these commands.

Pro-gay theologians argue that Leviticus 18:22 and 20:13 are specifically condemning participation in homosexual acts that were part of pagan worship, not homosexuality in general. For support, they note the Hebrew word used — *toevah*, which is translated "abomination" or "detestable" — is one that is directly associated with idolatry. So, they say, this proves that these passages about homosexuality are ultimately about God commanding the Israelites not to imitate the worship practices of other religions around them.

How do you respond to these questions and claims?

"Natural" and "Unnatural" Sex — Romans 1:24 – 32

In this passage the apostle Paul talks about people exchanging natural relations for unnatural ones, and it has been commonly held that he is referring to homosexual sex. However, critics argue that Paul is not talking about consensual homosexual sex between people who are naturally homosexual, but about straight people who are changing their nature and having homosexual sex.

They note that the context of Paul's comments are people who are practicing the worship of pagan religions in which participating in homosexual sex as a heterosexual was typical. Thus, they contend, if people are naturally gay and not having homosexual sex as part of idolatrous worship, then it's okay, because Paul was not condemning that.

How do you respond to these arguments?

Homosexual Prostitution Is the Sin, Not Homosexual Sex — 1 Corinthians 6:9 – 10; 1 Timothy 1:9 – 10

Similarly, pro-gay theologians argue that in these verses Paul condemns homosexual prostitution as a sin, but not consensual homosexual sex. They note that most Christians have no idea that the Greek word Paul used here is not the actual word for "homosexual" but the word *arsenokoitai*. The meaning of this word is unclear, as it is a word Paul seems to have originated (which seems to be true).

> ... Neither the sexually immoral nor idolaters nor adulterers nor male prostitutes [*malokois*] nor practicing homosexuals [*arsenokotai*] ...
>
> *I CORINTHIANS 6:9 TNIV*

In 1 Corinthians 6:9, the Greek word *malokois* proceeds the word *arsenokoitai*. *Malokois* means "soft" or "weak" and was often used to refer to the more passive males, usually young males who sold themselves for sex. So, these critics say, the verse refers to effeminate male prostitutes and those paying for sex with them, not homosexuals in general.

How would you answer this argument?

> ... for the sexually immoral, for those practicing homosexuality [*arsenokoitai*], for slave traders and liars and perjurers.
>
> *1 TIMOTHY 1:10 TNIV*

In 1 Timothy 1:10, the Greek word *arsenokoitai* is used again on its own. Because the meaning is not certain and there was actually another Greek word that Paul could have used for "homosexual" if he had wanted, critics opt for the same interpretation as for 1 Corinthians 6:19. They say that the sin being condemned is the hiring of someone for sex, not being homosexual.

How do you answer these claims?

Jesus Did Not Talk about Homosexuality

Another argument becoming more common today is that because Jesus did not talk about homosexuality or address it is as a sin, he must not have felt it was too important or even a sin at all.

How would you respond to this?

If you believe that the practice of homosexuality is a sin, then how would you respond to a Christian homosexual who is celibate? How do you think your church would respond?

> HUMAN SEXUALITY IS HOLISTIC SEXUALITY, NOT JUST FOCUSING ON HOMOSEXUALITY AND TELLING PEOPLE THEY SHOULDN'T HAVE SEX BEFORE MARRIAGE.
> *THEY LIKE JESUS BUT NOT THE CHURCH, P. 150*

WRAP-UP

Pray that instead of the church and Christians being known as homophobic, we will be known as a loving and welcoming community that holds to biblical guidelines.

May we move from being known as homophobic to → Being known as a loving and welcoming community that holds to biblical guidelines

HOW YOU CAN RESPOND

Choose at least one of the following suggested activities/reflections to complete over the next week. Consider sharing with your friends or small group members the impact the activity or reflection has on you.

1. Reexamine the passages on homosexuality in this session as well as others from your Bible. Are you ready to respond to the new ways of viewing the Scriptures as well as people's questions about them? You might even consider a dialogue at a future study, with a couple of group members taking on the role of question askers and the rest responding.

2. Do you know anyone who is gay? If you do, are you comfortable enough with them to ask them how they feel Christians, in general, have treated them?

3. Take time to reflect on whether you have a poor attitude toward homosexuals. The next time you find yourself with a poor attitude, remember the pain Penny went through and the many like her who have lost trust in Christians as a result.

4. Do you know what your church has to offer those who have same-sex attraction and desire to get biblical and loving guidance?

RECOMMENDED RESOURCES
FOR FURTHER STUDY

Welcoming but Not Affirming: An Evangelical Response To Homosexuality by Stanley Grenz, Westminster John Knox Press, 1998. A great book covering this issue from various depths and perspectives, yet through an evangelical lens.

Homosexuality and the Bible: Two Views by Robert A. J. Gagnon and Dan O. Via, Augsburg Fortress, 2003. One coauthor embraces pro-gay theology and the other a conservative view. Each author then critiques the other's arguments. A concise resource for knowing and understanding both sides of the debate.

Loving Homosexuals as Jesus Would: A Fresh Christian Approach by Chad W. Thompson, Brazos, 2004. This book by a guy in his twenties who struggled with same-sex attraction while growing up in the church is an eye-opener that illustrates how poorly prepared the church is to respond and minister to homosexuals.

www.lovinghomosexuals.com — The website of Chad Thompson.

www.soulforce.com — Dan Kimball does not agree with this website's theological beliefs regarding the practice of homosexuality. But the site is well worth visiting if only to better understand the arguments of pro-gay theology and to hear how Christians have at times wrongly hurt the homosexual community.

www.exodus–international.org — An organization and ministry that addresses homosexual issues.

www.robgagnon.net — Robert A. J. Gagnon, associate professor of New Testament at Pittsburgh Theological Seminary, has done extensive study on homosexuality within the biblical text. The website includes articles about the Bible and homosexuality.

DO CHRISTIANS ARROGANTLY THINK ALL OTHER RELIGIONS ARE WRONG?

"All I hear from Christians is that all other world religions are wrong and going to hell. I have tried to have an intelligent conversation with them about this and discuss the beauty in other expressions of spirituality, but they go into this religious rhetoric and avoid the hard questions. It seems they have programmed dogmatic answers that someone has told them, and they can't even hold any type of normal back and forth conversation about any other spiritual beliefs but theirs."

DUGGAN, IN THEY LIKE JESUS BUT NOT THE CHURCH, PP. 164–165

DVD SEGMENT #1

Let's watch as Dan Kimball introduces the growing awareness of other religions in our culture and then discusses the issue with Duggan.

DVD Notes
Interfaith retreat center

"What denomination are you?" vs. "What religion or religions are you?"

Examples from culture

The rising diversity of faith

Duggan's story

GROUP STUDY AND DISCUSSION #1

1. In what ways do you see the retreat center that Dan Kimball visited and the world religions game that Dan showed to be a portrait of what's going on in our emerging culture?

2. Where do you see examples of religious diversity in your own community or among people you know?

   Do you sense that people outside the church are experimenting and mixing various faiths or are they strongly and deeply committing to one specific faith?

Do you sense that even some people inside the church are accepting and open to faiths other than Christianity being equally true? If so, where have you seen this?

3. What stood out to you about Duggan's story?

4. Have you ever encountered a Christian who presented his or her faith like a "horse with blinders," as Duggan describes? Why do you think people present their faith this way? What do you think is the effect of this approach on non-Christians?

DVD SEGMENT #2

Let's watch as Dan Kimball discusses how Christians can respond to the rising awareness of other world religions.

DVD Notes
Lessons from Duggan

Think like a missionary

Explanation of diagrams

The role of apologetics

Knowing what you believe

GROUP STUDY AND DISCUSSION #2

1. The pop singer Madonna once said, "I do believe that all paths lead to god. It's a shame that we end up having religious wars, because so many of the messages are the same." How do you respond to statements like Madonna's and Duggan's—that all religions express truth and are basically the same?

Read the following excerpt and diagrams from Dan Kimball's book that will help you counter people's argument that all religions lead to God.

[When] people generally will say that all paths lead to God ... I draw a mountain and write "God" at the top. Then I draw various paths making their way up the mountain and label them "Christianity," "Islam," "Hinduism," and so on.

Then I explain that because this is an important idea, we should really take a look at each of the paths to see what the various faiths believe. I explain that in many ways this metaphor of God living on a mountaintop breaks down because God isn't limited to a mountaintop; he is everywhere. But then I keep going, since it is a way to visually make some sense of this common way of thinking about God and other faiths. After I draw a mountain, I ask the person to list some of the fundamental beliefs of each faith concerning who God is, who Jesus is, what salvation requires, and what each believes about the afterlife, and I'll jot them down, adding to the list if the person doesn't know much about the different faiths.

DO ALL PATHS LEAD TO GOD?

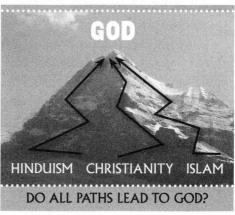

HINDUISM   CHRISTIANITY   ISLAM

DO ALL PATHS LEAD TO GOD?

For the purpose of this book, I'll give a simplified version, but basi-cally I explain that according to the Hindu path:

God: there are many gods (thousands of them)

Jesus: could be one of many gods but is not the only way

Afterlife: reincarnation to pay off karmic debt, eventually becoming one with the impersonal Brahman

So the path of Hinduism leads to a mountaintop where there are thousands of gods.

Then I explain that according to the Islamic path:

God: one God, Allah

Jesus: a prophet but not the Son of God

Afterlife: paradise or hell; salvation is based on weighing the good and the bad done in life

So on this mountaintop there is one God, but Allah is different from the Hindu gods, and, as we will see, different from the Christian God.

And then according to the Christian path:

God: one God (Father, Son, Holy Spirit)

Jesus: the Son of God, the way to salvation

Afterlife: heaven or hell, based not on anything we do but on whether we have faith in Jesus

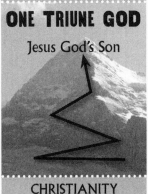

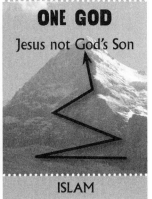

I explain that when you look at various world faiths at a base level, in most cases, you do see similarities. For example, most faiths teach that we should love one another and love our neighbors as ourselves. Because more and more people are familiar with Buddhism, I generally will point out that Buddha and Jesus both taught similar sayings. Jesus said, "Do to others as you would have them do to you" (Luke 6:31), and Buddha said, "Consider others as yourself" (Dhammapada 10:1). In my hand-drawn diagrams, I usually circle the commonalities among the beliefs I've listed at the bases of the mountains, and I draw some paths intersecting at the bases to show that there can be similarities at this level.

But then I explain that after you move past these base-level teachings, continuing up the paths of what each world faith believes, you arrive at the top and find that each world faith takes you to an entirely different mountaintop. Because most people who claim that all roads lead to God or that all paths lead to the same mountaintop don't usually look too deeply into the beliefs of each religion, their conclusion is only superficial. If they looked into each one, they would see drastic and contradictory differences between them. I explain that they all lead to different mountaintops. I usually also explain that while often only Christianity gets a bad rap for exclusivity and its belief in hell, most other faiths also claim to be the only true way, and there

77

are various forms of hell in many other faiths as well. Most people I talk to don't know that.

So when we actually study world religions, we see that it's not the case that all roads lead to God, because you cannot have God saying he is one God, as in Islam and Christianity, but have thousands of gods in Hinduism. And you can't say that Jesus is the Son of God and the Savior, as Christianity teaches, but then have Islam say Jesus is just a prophet. These beliefs are different and even contradictory. Explaining this to people who have never really thought it through leads to the question, So which one is true? When it comes to the fundamental teachings of the various world faiths, either they are all wrong, or only one is right. They can't all be true.

In all of the times I have taken people through this process, I have never once had someone say, "This doesn't matter. Everything is relative and they can all be right." Usually it catches them off-guard because they never viewed it like this before. But time and time again, I don't get counterarguments once it is explained like this. Despite what you read about our relativistic world and the impact of postmodernism, when you logically and gently lay the facts out for people, there's not too much arguing. People see the contradiction and aren't afraid to say that it seems like all paths can't lead to the same God. At this point, nothing has been proved, but the question is raised, Why do Christians believe they are the right path? This is where apologetics and logic come in. This is where we need an apologetic for why we believe the Bible is inspired and true. This is when we can speak of Jesus' resurrection and how he has changed our lives. Since they know us and trust us, our words have far more impact and meaning when we share.

2. Address the idea from the preceding excerpt (pages 75 – 78) that all religions share some base-level truth. Do you agree or disagree that there is some truth in most world religions? How might this "common ground" help you when interacting with someone who has a more pluralistic belief system?

3. The excerpt pointed out some similar sayings of Jesus and Buddha. Did you also realize that both Buddha and Jesus had similar temptation-in-the-wilderness experiences? How would you respond to these similarities in the story of Buddha and the story of Jesus?

4. Do you know of any other, similar stories from other religions that parallel the stories in the Bible?

5. Christians believe that Jesus is the one and only way to God. Can you list at least five Bible verses that back up that belief? *(See appendix, page 129, for suggested answers.)*

   1)

   2)

   3)

   4)

   5)

6. Do you ever struggle with the claim of Christianity that Jesus is the only way to salvation? Why or why not?

I'M NOT SAYING THAT WE NEED TO KEEP QUIET ABOUT THE EXCLUSIVE CLAIMS OF JESUS. QUITE THE OPPOSITE, ACTUALLY. BUT IN SOME CASES OUR HEARTS AND ATTITUDES NEED TO CHANGE IN HOW WE TALK TO PEOPLE ABOUT THE CLAIMS OF JESUS.

THEY LIKE JESUS BUT NOT THE CHURCH, P. 170

In the DVD, Duggan expressed that Christians he has met have not been able to articulate too much about other faiths, and this shows disrespect to someone like him. Read the following diagram to get a basic sense for the development of world faiths. *(There's a more visual rendering of this information in the appendix, pages 130–131.)*

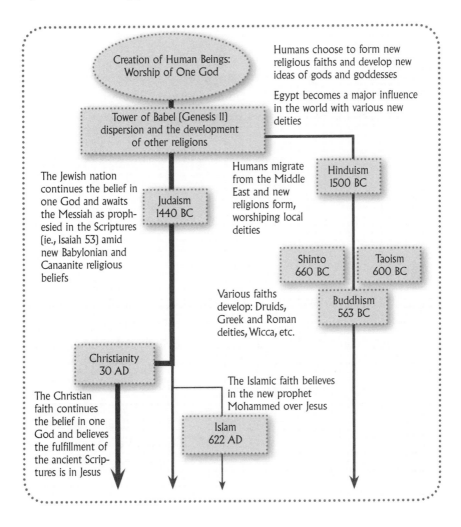

7. How would you explain the differences between messages of faith to someone using the diagram on page 81?

8. Read Exodus 20:3. Why do you think this is the first commandment? Is it possible to keep a healthy and humble attitude toward other faiths yet still keep this commandment? Explain.

WRAP-UP

Pray that instead of the church and Christians being known for arrogantly claiming that all other religions are wrong, we will be known for respecting other people who hold different beliefs and lovingly ready to share with them why we believe that Jesus is the way, the truth, and the life.

May we move from being known as arrogantly thinking all religions but ours are wrong to

Treating others who have different beliefs with respect while strongly claiming Jesus as the way, the truth, and the life

HOW YOU CAN RESPOND

Choose at least one of the following suggested activities/reflections to complete over the next week. Consider sharing with your friends or small group members the impact the activity or reflection has on you.

1. Review the mountaintop diagrams that Dan presented in this session. In sharing your faith, it's important to acknowledge that at a base level, there may be some truth in most religions, such as "love your neighbor" or "do not murder." But when examining each religion more deeply, the last diagram (page 77) reveals that at the top of each mountain there is a different "god" or "gods." All religions are *not* the same. Exploring the primary doctrines and beliefs of the various faiths only serves to illustrate that they contradict and clash with each other in very significant ways.

   Spend some time thinking about how you would explain this idea to someone in your own words. Then practice drawing the mountaintop diagram on your own, or perhaps at the next group meeting.

2. Review the world faiths timetable diagram on page 81 as well as the world map diagrams in the appendix on pages 130–131. Practice sketching one of these two concepts on your own, and also consider explaining it to someone in your group before the next meeting. They are excellent yet simple visual tools to illustrate to a non-Christian the concept that history started with belief in one God, then over time other faiths developed and spread throughout the globe.

3. Buy or borrow one of the books listed in the recommended resources on page 84 and read it to get a better understanding of the development of world faiths. You don't have to be an expert, but in our culture today it helps tremendously to at least have a basic understanding of other faiths, especially when conversing with a member of one of those faiths.

4. The next time you have a spiritual dialogue with someone of another faith, remember to listen to them as you expect them to listen to you. It demonstrates you care enough about that person to want to understand his or her beliefs.

RECOMMENDED RESOURCES
FOR FURTHER STUDY

The Compact Guide to World Religions by Dean C. Halverson, Bethany, 1996. An easy-to-understand guide to world religions from an evangelical perspective. The hardcover edition includes many helpful photos.

Is Jesus the Only Savior? by James R. Edwards, Eerdmans, 2005. An excellent book that discusses the claim of Jesus being the only Savior among other religions and beliefs.

The Case for the Real Jesus by Lee Strobel, Zondervan, 2007, and *Lord or Legend?: Wrestling with the Jesus Dilemma* by Gregory Boyd and Paul Rhodes Eddy, Baker, 2007. Both of these books explore from an evangelical perspective the criticisms that Christianity borrowed from other religions.

www.beliefnet.com — A non-Christian website that presents information and perspectives on both major and minor world religions, including Christianity.

ARE CHRISTIANS FUNDAMENTALISTS WHO TAKE THE WHOLE BIBLE LITERALLY?

"Christians seem really silly with some of the fundamentalist views they have. They take apart the Bible and pull out the verses that they want to shame people with. They take Jesus' words and then embellish them and give meaning to them in order to control the people in the way they want to."

MAYA, IN THEY LIKE JESUS BUT NOT THE CHURCH, P.188

DVD SEGMENT #1

In this final session, let's watch as Dan Kimball introduces the idea that Christians are often seen today as closed-minded fundamentalists who blindly take the whole Bible literally. In this segment, Dan also talks with Dustan about his faith journey.

DVD Notes
Loving the God-breathed Bible

Criticism of the Bible

The green notebook

Contradictions

Sticker

Dustan

Similarity of the stories in the Bible and other religions

GROUP STUDY AND DISCUSSION #1

1. Dan Kimball says, "There's an increasing amount of teaching that the Bible is not inspired." Where have you seen this statement played out? How would you define "inspired"?

2. Have you ever encountered a "green notebook" situation with someone? What happened? What was your response? What was the outcome?

3. Why do you think these tougher issues from the Bible sometimes go unaddressed in the church? What are the tougher issues that you feel get ignored?

4. In the DVD, Dustan said that Christians don't really do their homework and look into why they believe what they do or study the origins of the Bible and how it was put together. In what ways do you agree with this statement? In what ways do you disagree?

5. Why do you think some people have the perception that Christians "step into a whole way of life and belief systems that they know nothing about?" Is this perception true?

6. Dustan shared how he discovered many things about other religions that he was never told growing up in church: for instance, pagan religions that predate Christianity had stories of the killing of a god and his resurrection, a virgin birth, having twelve followers, and so on, and Christianity merely included these pagan elements in the New Testament to deify Jesus. What would you say to Dustan, who has read these very claims in books by respected university professors and historical scholars? *(See appendix, pages 133–134, for answers.)*

DVD SEGMENT #2

Let's watch as Dan Kimball discusses why we need to become thoughtful theologians when sharing our faith.

DVD Notes

Knowing what you believe

Are you a fundamentalist?

The original five fundamentalist beliefs

Bible study skills

Articulating your faith

GROUP STUDY AND DISCUSSION #2

1. List at least three verses from the Bible that claim God inspired it in its entirety. *(See appendix, page 134, for suggested answers.)*

   1)

   2)

   3)

2. Using verses from the Bible to claim its inspiration could be called circular reasoning. That's why it's important to have some reasons in addition to the Bible's own claims about itself that you can use to prove its trustworthiness. Remember, Dustan indicated that most Christians didn't even know how the Bible was put together and why or why not it can be trusted.

List five solid reasons why you have confidence that the Bible is inspired and trustworthy. *(See appendix, pages 134–135, for suggested answers.)*

1)

2)

3)

4)

5)

3. It is important to know and be able to briefly explain how the Bible was canonized (each book officially accepted as Scripture). Can you share the basic story of how the formation of the Bible occurred and how the books were selected for inclusion? Can you list some of the reasons you believe that the compiled books of the Bible are the ones that God wanted and that the ones left out were under dispute? *(See appendix, pages 135–137, for suggested answer.)*

4. How would you answer the question about whether or not you take the whole Bible literally?

Read the following excerpt from Dan Kimball's book, then answer the remaining questions.

The word *literal* conjures images of people who think we should accept everything in the Bible as literal. But figurative language isn't literal. If we say that someone is green with envy, we don't mean his skin is green. Similarly, the Bible says things that aren't meant to be taken literally. They should be understood as figurative language used to convey truth. For example, Jesus said some true things about himself using figurative language. He called himself bread (John 6:35) and a gate (John 10:7). He called people sheep (Matt. 10:6). Obviously he didn't mean these things literally. The Bible uses figures of speech such as similes and metaphors to make comparisons. When Jesus said, "The kingdom of heaven is like a mustard seed, which a man took and planted in a field" (Matt. 13:31), he didn't mean that the kingdom literally is a mustard seed. When the Bible says, "The trees of the field will clap their hands" (Isa. 55:12), it doesn't mean that the trees literally will clap actual hands. Jesus used hyperbole to make a point when he said, "If your right eye causes you to sin, gouge it out" (Matt. 5:29). He did not mean that you should actually pluck out your eye. Other times the Bible uses anthropomorphisms, describing God in human terms: "For the eyes of the Lord are on the righteous and his ears are attentive to their prayer, but the face of the Lord is against those who do evil" (1 Peter 3:12). But this doesn't mean that God has a physical face with eyes and ears. The book of Revelation and parts of the books of Daniel, Isaiah, Ezekiel, and Zechariah are written in apocalyptic form, using visions, symbols, and numbers to communicate. Because most of the apocalyptic works were written during times of persecution, the writers used symbols that were understood by the persecuted but not by the persecutors. These apocalyptic sections of Scripture had true meaning but were not meant to be taken literally. So as leaders in the church, we have to be careful how we teach and what conclusions we make. The people in our churches follow our lead and will learn from our teaching how to study and approach the Bible.

5. Although the entire Bible is 100 percent inspired, as we just read, it is written in several genres. So we actually don't take it all literally, because it was not all written to be taken literally.

   In the space that follows provide a quick definition of each term in relation to the Bible and, in the case of the final five, an example from Scripture. *(See appendix, pages 137–139, for suggested responses.)*

Literal =

Figurative =

Metaphor =

Hyperbole =

Anthropomorphism =

Apocalyptic =

6. List the original "five fundamentals" of the Christian faith. *(See appen-dix, page 139, for answers.)*

1)

2)

3)

4)

5)

How was the word *fundamentalist* originally used, and how it is used today?

Is there anything wrong with having fundamentalist beliefs?

After watching this DVD segment, do you consider yourself a "funda-mentalist" (even if you don't use the word)? Why or why not?

EXAMPLES OF CORE BELIEFS	EXAMPLES OF NON-CORE BELIEFS
• Inspiration of Scripture	• The length of time for creation
• Deity of Jesus	• Tastes in clothing, music, movies
• Virgin birth	• Drinking alcohol
• The resurrection of Jesus	• How Jesus will return
• The future return of Jesus	• How election and free will work
• Salvation through Jesus alone	• Which gifts of the Spirit are for today
• Atonement for sin	• Worship styles
• God is triune—Father, Son, Spirit	• Preaching styles
• Fruit of the Spirit should be evident in our lives	• Role of women in the church
• Covenant of marriage	
• Serving those in need	
• Future judgment	

7. Consider the chart of core beliefs and non-core beliefs on page 96. Do you find yourself focusing more on the core beliefs or the non-core beliefs when disagreeing with someone? How is your heart toward people who have different non-core beliefs than you? Are there beliefs you would add to or remove from either list?

WRAP-UP

Pray that instead of being known as fundamentalists who take the whole Bible literally without thinking, we will be known as a people who are thoughtful theologians, diligently studying and living out the truths of the Scriptures.

> May we move from being known as fundamentalists who take the whole Bible literally without thinking to → Being known as a people who are thoughtful theologians, who diligently study and live out the inspired truths of Scripture

HOW YOU CAN RESPOND

Choose at least one of the following suggested activities/reflections to complete in the coming days.

1. Make a list of your core beliefs regarding your faith. Which are fundamental doctrines? Which are more based on opinion? Now mark those that are more likely to come up in discussions and conversations. Are you ever tempted to teach your opinions as Bible truths? How can you distinguish opinion from fundamental beliefs?

2. When you are listening to a sermon, studying the Bible, or even quoting a Bible verse, do you spend adequate time looking at the background of the book, when it was written, to whom it was written, and the cultural context of the time it was written? Do you "do your homework," as Dustan suggested? Do the pastors who are preaching the sermons you listen to seem to be doing their homework?

    If you do not own any commentary or study helps, research and begin developing a library of books to help you "do your homework." Books are worth the investment when it comes to becoming a better student of Scripture.

3. What are some unusual verses/passages/stories from the Bible that you have struggled with or wondered how to understand? As an assignment, take one of the problematic Scriptures and begin studying it more deeply, with the goal of better understanding it.

4. The next time someone outside of the church asks you about a problematic Bible passage, don't just ignore their question or become defensive. Take up the challenge and "do your homework" to give them an answer. And don't be afraid to admit to the fact that there may be some verses that are too difficult to understand from a human perspective. That does not negate the Bible as the inspired Word of God. It just means there are some unusual things in Scripture that are hard to grasp in our culture, but they were understood when they were written and God knows what they mean.

RECOMMENDED RESOURCES
FOR FURTHER STUDY

The following books and websites expertly discuss why we can trust the Scriptures in the face of much criticism.

Reinventing Jesus by J. Ed Komoszewski, M. James Sawyer, and Daniel B. Wallace, Kregel, 2006

The Missing Gospels: Unearthing the Truth behind Alternative Christianities by Darrell L. Bock, Thomas Nelson, 2006

Misquoting Truth: A Guide to the Fallacies of Bart Ehrman's "Misquoting Jesus" by Timothy Paul Jones, InterVarsity Press, 2007

The Case for Christ by Lee Strobel, Zondervan, 1998

The Case for the Real Jesus by Lee Strobel, Zondervan 2007

The Politically Incorrect Guide to the Bible by Robert J. Hutchinson, Regnery, 2007

www.bible.org—This site answers many tough biblical questions from a conservative viewpoint.

www.jesuscreed.org—This is the weblog of North Park University professor and theologian Scot McKnight, who is constantly raising critical issues to think about.

The following books help readers discover the joy of personal Bible study and how to develop Bible study skills.

Grasping God's Word: A Hands-On Approach to Reading, Interpreting, and Applying the Bible by J. Scott Duvall and J. Daniel Hays, Zondervan, 2005

Epiphany: Discover the Delight of God's Word by Chuck Smith Jr., WaterBrook, 2003

CLOSING THOUGHTS AND PRAYER

By Dan Kimball

I
t is very difficult to address these highly sensitive issues in a six-session study with just an hour or so together each meeting. So I imagine that some of these discussions may have raised more questions than they answered. But to me that is actually a good thing, for my hope is that your curiosity will force you to pursue further study. Be sure to take advantage of the book and Internet resources I have recommended throughout this participant's guide.

But studying simply to better understand our culture's perceptions of the church isn't an end in itself. My ultimate hope and prayer is that we actually get to *speak* about these things to those who like Jesus but not the church. Perhaps like me, you have discovered you're caught in the Christian bubble. When I realized my predicament, I had to intentionally put myself in places to be able to meet people outside of the church. Usually for me, it was connecting with people of similar musical tastes, as music is something I can easily talk about. For you, it might be sports or a book club or a school committee. It might as simple as inviting some non-Christian neighbors to dinner or switching from a Christian friend who cuts your hair to someone who isn't a Christian so you can get to know some people you wouldn't have met otherwise. We encounter all types of people every day. Ask God to show you who he might want you to befriend.

Let me reiterate two important points I mentioned at the start of this study. One, never forget that it is the power of the gospel—not apologetics—that changes lives. Yes, like any effective missionary, we need to be active in our culture—listening to people, befriending people, praying for people. We definitely need to be ready to give an answer for the hope that we have to those who ask us — and I hope these sessions have helped you do that. But it is God's Spirit who will ultimately pierce people's hearts and make them realize their need to put faith in the biblical Jesus. So please continue to pray for those you have identified who may like Jesus but not the church. And pray that God will bring other people into your life who don't yet know the biblical Jesus. I can't imagine that is a prayer God won't answer.

My second reminder: don't forget that you can't *like* Jesus, but *not like* the church. The church is the bride of Jesus — a beautiful thing; he loves and honors the church despite our weaknesses and even when we don't honor him. People need the church because the church is how Jesus designed us to function — not alone, but in community.

The words of author Henri Nouwen ring true here:

> When we have been wounded by the Church, our temptation is to reject it. But when we reject the Church it becomes very hard for us to keep in touch with the living Christ. When we say, "I love Jesus, but I hate the Church," we end up losing not only the Church but Jesus too. The challenge is to forgive the Church.
>
> This challenge is especially great because the Church seldom asks us for forgiveness, at least not officially. But the Church as an often fallible human organization needs our forgiveness, while the Church as the living Christ among us continues to offer us forgiveness.
>
> It is important to think about the Church not as "over there" but as a community of struggling, weak people of whom we are part and in whom we meet our Lord and Redeemer.
>
> From *Bread for the Journey: A Daybook of Wisdom and Faith* (San Francisco: HarperCollins, 1996), entry for October 27th: "Forgiving the Church"

There are countless numbers of people who like Jesus but not the church. What is so incredibly hopeful is that they truly are open to discussing Jesus. They truly are open to discussing our apologetic about what Jesus' church really is, allowing us to clear up any misperceptions they may have. They truly are open to receiving an apology for how we in the church have misrepresented Jesus and his church. They truly are open to even forgiving the church where forgiveness is needed. But they need to hear that apologetic and apology from someone they can *trust*.

Jesus said he will build his church (Matt. 16:13–18) and we are the ones he sends on that important mission (Matt. 28:19–20). But being on a mission means not just sitting around in our comfortable, cozy Christian bubble. So my closing prayer for all of us is this:

May our hearts be so grateful for what Jesus has done for us and for the joy we experience in knowing him that we will do whatever it takes to break out of the Christian bubble and share him with others. May we serve gladly on the mission of Jesus, and may God use us to help people discover that they can not only like Jesus, but that they can love Jesus and love his church as well.

Amen.

The forthcoming book, *Do You Like Jesus but Not the Church?* is designed to explore the six session topics covered in this book, but with more depth. Not only will it help you express answers to people's questions and perceptions about the church and Christianity, it is written with tone and terminology to be able to give to someone who likes Jesus but not the church. For more information, visit the website: *www.theylikejesus.com*.

APPENDIX

SUGGESTED ANSWERS TO CROSS-REFERENCED QUESTIONS IN EACH SESSION

SESSION 1:
THE DANGER OF
THE CHRISTIAN BUBBLE

GROUP STUDY AND DISCUSSION #1

4. John 17:15 – 18. EXTRA: What do you think Jesus meant in this passage by "the world"? What do you think he meant by "evil"?

The word for "world" used here is the Greek word *kosmos*. The "world" generally means the human-centered philosophies and systems of thinking and values that go against what it means to be a disciple and follower of Jesus. Some of the world's philosophies can even be anti-Christian. We see this described in 1 John 2:15 – 16 (TNIV): "Do not love the world or anything in the world. If you love the world, love for the Father is not in you. For everything in the world — the cravings of sinful people, the lust of their eyes and their boasting about what they have and do — comes not from the Father but from the world." The Scriptures also teach that the "world" is controlled by the evil one (1 John 5:19).

However, Scripture also says that God loves the "world" (John 3:16) and that Jesus prayed that his followers would remain "in the world" (John 17:15 – 18). So there seems to be a contradiction here. What resolves this apparent dilemma is understanding that the word "world" in these passages refers to different things. When we read that God loves the world, it means he loves the people, not the human-centered philosophies and values that are counterbiblical.

The "world" Jesus speaks of here in John 17 is people. We *should not* isolate ourselves from nonbelievers, hide from culture, and create a Christian bubble; we *should* be out in culture among the people whom God loves (John 3:16). At the same time, we are to be careful not to fall into "evil," the world systems and philosophies that would draw us away from Jesus. It is a balance we have to carefully walk, but as citizens of the kingdom of heaven (Phil. 3:20), we can be *in* the world but not *of* the world.

Consider also these verses:

> "In the same way, let your light shine before others, that they may see your good deeds and glorify your Father in heaven."
>
> *MATTHEW 5:16 TNIV*

> Live such good lives among the pagans that, though they accuse you of doing wrong, they may see your good deeds and glorify God on the day he visits us.
>
> *1 PETER 2:12*

In order for our "light to shine," in order for people to "see our good deeds and glorify God," we need to be in relationships where they can experience this. Following the example of Jesus and his disciples, we can be friends with those who are not (yet) Christians and part of their lives, but refuse to participate in certain activities (Matt. 9:10–13).

GROUP STUDY AND DISCUSSION #2

3. **How would you describe the biblical Jesus? What may be the difference between the pop-culture version of Jesus and the biblical Jesus? What are key things about Jesus biblically that everyone should know?**

There is a pop-culture version of Jesus that pictures him more like a first-century Gandhi or Martin Luther King Jr. Some people may like this "Jesus," but it is different Jesus than the Jesus of the Scriptures.

How would you describe Jesus to someone who is unaware or fuzzy as to who he truly is? Dan Kimball describes him as follows in the book *They Like Jesus but Not the Church* (pages 56–57):

> When I think of Jesus, I think of the triune God, who eternally exists in three persons — Father, Son, and Holy Spirit — coeternal in being, coeternal in nature, coequal in power and glory, all three persons having the same attributes and perfections (Deut. 6:4; 2 Cor. 13:14). These terms may sound technical to people,

but these ideas are so incredibly hard to grasp that technical words sometimes convey them better than emotional responses. I think of Jesus as the one who was conceived by the Holy Spirit and born of the Virgin Mary (Luke 1:26–31). He was a Jewish rabbi (John 1:38), a teacher who astonished people with his insight and his authoritative teaching (Matt. 7:28–29). I think of his heart breaking with compassion for people (Matt. 9:36) and how he wept for people, even for those who rejected him (Luke 19:41). I think of the Jesus who was an advocate for the poor, the marginalized, and the oppressed (Luke 4:18–19; Matt. 19:16–30; Luke14:13; Matt. 25:31–46). I think of the one who stood strong against the religious legalism of his day (Luke 20:19–20). I think of the one who not only drank wine but also provided it (John 2:1–11). I think of the one who didn't just sit in a holy huddle or point out the wrongs of culture but hung out with sinners and ate with them (Matt. 9:10). I think of the Jesus who was tempted and understands temptation yet was sinless (Heb. 4:15; 1 Peter 1:22). I think of the Jesus who was sent by God because of his great love for humanity to take on our sin (John 1:1–2, 14, 29; 3:16–21). I think of the Jesus who accomplished our redemption through his death on the cross as a substitutionary sacrifice and then was bodily resurrected from the dead (Rom. 3:24; 1 Peter 2:24). I think of the Jesus who appeared to his disciples and said that they have a mission not to create an inwardly focused community and to complain about the world but rather to go out and with the power of the Spirit live missional lives, bringing the light of Jesus to others (Acts 1:8). I think of the Jesus who sees the church as his bride (Rev. 21:2, 9) and loves the church, even when we disappoint him. I think of the Jesus who ascended into heaven and is now exalted at the right hand of God, where, as our High Priest, he intercedes for us and serves as our advocate (Acts 1:9–10; Heb. 7:25; 9:24). I also think, soberly, of the Jesus who will one day come again to judge the living and the dead (1 Peter 4:5; Rom. 14:9; 2 Tim. 4:1). Jesus is our friend and the friend of sinners, but he also is a righteous judge who will hold us all accountable one day for how we lived our lives. We must have a balanced view of Jesus, being careful not to swing to one extreme or the other.

The reason I am writing this book, the reason I continue to go out of my way to befriend, meet, hang out with, and talk with those who like Jesus but not the church is because I so desire for others to experience the full Jesus, not just the good teacher or the friend but also the Lord of Lords and King of Kings and the Savior who changes lives.

EXTRA: As trust is built in any relationship with a non-Christian, the need to articulate the gospel will eventually arise. Can you define "the gospel"? What Bible passages would you turn to?

"The Greek word translated as gospel means *'a reward for bringing good news'* or simply *'good news.'* In Isaiah 40:9, the prophet proclaimed the 'good tidings' that God would rescue His people from captivity. In His first sermon in Nazareth, Jesus used a passage from the Old Testament to characterize the spirit of His ministry: 'The Spirit of the Lord is upon me, because he has anointed me to preach the gospel to the poor' (Luke 4:18).

"The gospel is not a new plan of salvation; it is the fulfillment of God's plan of salvation which was begun in Israel, was completed in Jesus Christ, and is made known by the church.

"The gospel is the saving work of God in His Son Jesus Christ and a call to faith in Him (Rom. 1:16–17). Jesus is more than a messenger of the gospel; He is the gospel. The good news of God was present in His life, teaching, and atoning death. Therefore, the gospel is both a historical event and a personal relationship." (*Nelson's Illustrated Bible Dictionary*, ed. Herbert Lockyer, Thomas Nelson Publishers, 1986)

Some Bible passages that help define the gospel:

- John 3:16
- Romans 1:16–17; 3:23; 6:23; 10:19–20
- 1 Corinthians 15:1–4

SESSION 2:
IS THE CHURCH NEGATIVE, JUDGMENTAL, AND POLITICAL?

GROUP STUDY AND DISCUSSION # 2

1. **A verse often quoted is Matthew 7:1 in which Jesus instructed, "Do not judge." What do you think Jesus specifically meant here — that no one will be judged or that Christians should not "judge" other people?**

   This statement of Jesus occurs in his Sermon on the Mount where he takes to task the hypocritcal religious leaders of the day (see, for example, Matt. 6:2, 5, 16). These men made judgments on others with a critical heart and condescending spirit and based on their own opinions and wrong motivations. Jesus tells his hearers — and us — that judging someone like this without caring for the person is wrong, that judging someone by human standards (outward appearances) and opinions instead of by the Scriptures is wrong. Only God truly knows what's in someone's heart. Jesus says that our hearts should be broken and filled with humility when making any judgment on another, because we are all guilty of something.

   However, Scripture notes many examples of calling out sin in other Christians. In 1 Corinthians 5:4–5, for example, we see the apostle Paul taking a public stand on the issue of immorality within the Corinthian church. In Galatians 2:11, we see him correcting Peter personally about a certain teaching. And he instructs Timothy to take a stand against false teaching in the church in Ephesus (1 Tim. 1:3–7). The apostle John also makes a similar warning (2 John 8–11).

But we have biblical guidelines for this type of "judging." Jesus himself instructed believers about correcting other believers when they are in intentional sin (Matt. 18:15–17). Galatians 6:1–5 offers additional guidance on confronting sin, with the goal of restoring the person. The Scriptures teach that church leaders should be open to correction (1 Tim. 5:19–20) and that friends should sharpen one another with corrective criticism (Prov. 27:6, 17).

Bottom line, Jesus taught that we should not rush to judge others without knowing their hearts, nor should we judge with an arrogant or condemning spirit. Jesus did not say to ignore sin ("anything goes"), but he (and other writers of Scripture) gave instruction on how to lovingly confront it. How we do it makes all the difference.

EXTRA: As the topic of tattoos came up in Dan's and Gary's remarks, are you aware of the Bible verse some Christians use to judge that tattoos are inappropriate?

Leviticus 19:28 says, "Do not cut your bodies for the dead or put tattoo marks on yourselves. I am the LORD." However, the context in which this verse was written is God speaking to Israel, specifically telling them to stay away from the religious practices of neighboring people groups. Note the surrounding verses, in which you'll also find prohibitions against eating bloody meat (v. 26), fortune-telling (v. 26), and cutting one's hair a certain way (v. 27)—all habits of those who practiced false religions.

As long as someone today gets tattoos as a form of body art and is not doing so as an act of worship to a false god, we really cannot use Leviticus 19:28 to make a case *not* to get a tattoo. It would be like saying a person can't sing in a church gathering because in cults and false religions they also sang songs when they met. We need to be careful not to make a judgment just because we might be personally uncomfortable with something, whether a tattoo or anything else. It is very easy to turn our opinions or uneasiness into judgments that are not based on Scripture.

3. **The apostle Paul taught the Corinthian church that there is a difference between judging Christians and judging those outside the church. Read 1 Corinthians 5:12–13. Who does it say should judge those outside the church? Who does it say should judge those inside the church? What is the difference between the two?**

Very clearly here the Scriptures say we have no right to judge those outside the church. Too often Christians spend time judging these people and their actions, when the Scriptures teach that right belongs to God alone. We often unrealistically expect non-Christians to act and be like Christians, then judge them if they don't live up to our personal expectations. It's only to be expected that non-Christians, without the instruction of Scripture or the guidance of the Holy Spirit, have some unique values and act differently than we do.

However, the Scriptures *do* say we should judge (with a good heart and within biblical guidelines) other Christians if they are clearly in unrepentant sin. See my comments for session two, question 1.

SESSION 3:
DOES THE CHURCH RESTRICT AND OPPRESS WOMEN?

GROUP STUDY AND DISCUSSION #2

3. Read 1 Corinthians 14:34–35 and 1 Timothy 2:11–15 aloud and then discuss how you would explain these passages. Imagine looking a twenty-five-year-old, well-educated female in the eyes as you read them.

These passages can raise all kinds of questions about the role of women in the church. In fact, the reason there is more than one viewpoint on this issue is because passages like these are not easy to understand. But if you have a personal conviction on the role of women in the church, then you need to have the integrity to at least be able to explain why you believe what you do.

The purpose of this study is not to exegete these passages fully — that wouldn't be possible in this brief session. Nor is the purpose of this study to debate the various interpretations. (There are recommended resources listed at the end of the session to help you explore further.)

We need to also remember that though the egalitarians and complementarians believe differently, they each take the Bible seriously and hold to its authority. There are godly, Spirit-filled Christian scholars, pastors, and church members on both sides of the debate. Often we have been taught only one particular viewpoint in our church and overlook other credible viewpoints. What's more, the issue isn't necessarily as black-and-white as we may have thought.

The two Scriptures given here to read are two of the most controversial and debated passages on the role of women:

> Women should remain silent in the churches. They are not allowed to speak, but must be in submission, as the law says. If they want to inquire about something, they should ask their own husbands at home; for it is disgraceful for a woman to speak in the church.
>
> *1 CORINTHIANS 14:34–35*

> A woman should learn in quietness and full submission. I do not permit a woman to teach or to have authority over a man; she must be silent. For Adam was formed first, then Eve. And Adam was not the one deceived; it was the woman who was deceived and became a sinner. But women will be saved through childbearing—if they continue in faith, love and holiness with propriety.
>
> *1 TIMOTHY 2:11–15*

Even complementarian churches don't seem to follow the 1 Corinthians 14 instructions to the extent that females cannot say anything within a worship gathering and must wait to go home to ask their husbands any questions. In complementarian churches females *do* speak and sing and aren't totally silent. And even complementarian churches don't typically teach that women are not saved unless they have a child, as a surface reading of 1 Timothy 2 seems to indicate. However, many do hold that women aren't allowed to teach men in any circumstance.

How would an egalitarian and a complementarian explain these verses to our hypothetical twenty-five-year-old female?

An *egalitarian* would look at these passages and state that most likely Paul is restricting women from teaching because in the first century women were typically uneducated. It was common in meetings at that time for educated listeners to be able to ask questions during teaching times, but it was considered inappropriate for the uneducated to do so. Paul was not saying this is mandatory for all churches and all women of all time, but was talking about a specific church's situation at that time.

An egalitarian would also raise the strong possibility that 1 Timothy 2:12 is speaking out against specific women who were abusing privileges and causing disruption in the specific church Paul was addressing—Ephesus. The city of Ephesus was known for its temple to Artemis, a Greek/Roman goddess; the theory is that perhaps women (who held authority in that pagan religious practice) were disrupting the church meeting either intentionally or out of ignorance and thus were instructed not to continue that behavior. Later in this epistle (1 Tim. 5:11–15), Paul referred to a group of women who were disruptive to the church through their attitudes and behaviors.

A *complementarian* would not necessarily agree with the egalitarian interpretations because nowhere in the New Testament does it specifically mention educational status as being the reason for women not to speak or teach in church. If education were a qualification for ministry, the majority of Jesus' disciples would have been disqualified. Because the Scriptures are silent about this, a complementarian would feel the egalitarian explanation is more speculative than factual. However, most complementarian churches do not take their conclusion to the extreme that women cannot speak at all in a church. They interpret the passages as women (or men) not being disruptive in a worship gathering. So a woman or a man can speak in a worship gathering as long as she or he is not disruptive and as long as the female is not the authoritative teacher over a man.

An *egalitarian* also believes that women are able to teach and be pastors or elders in churches. Though egalitarians would admit that male leaders were the cultural norm in Scripture, they point to several passages that indicate women were spiritual leaders or prophetesses too, for instance:

- Miriam (Ex. 15:20; Mic. 6:4)
- Deborah (Judg. 4:4–7)
- Philip's four daughters (Acts 21:8–9)
- Females prophesying (1 Cor. 11:5)

They also cite other examples of women serving in teaching or leadership roles, including the following:

- Junia (Rom. 16:7)—This historically has been translated as a male name, but scholars now are leaning toward this being a female who was listed as an "apostle."

- Phoebe (Rom. 16:1)—Called a "servant (deacon) of the church." The word for "deacon" used here (*diakonon*) is the male version of the word, which could mean that Phoebe was seen as the lead deacon.
- Priscilla (Acts 18:24–26)—A teacher. It is unusual to see the female name listed first when a male and female are spoken of together. This may indicate Priscilla's role was more prominent than her husband Aquila's.
- Mary mother of John (Acts 12:12)—Seemed to be the overseer of a house church.
- Lydia (Acts 16:14–15)—Overseer of a house church.
- Laborers equally together in the work (Rom. 16:12; Phil. 4:2–3)

Overall, the *egalitarian* viewpoint stresses the biblical record that men and women equally bear God's image (Gen. 1:27) and that his original intention was for man and woman to be coequal in their roles and share responsibility. However, the fall (Gen. 3) introduced inequality into their relationship, and since then, there has been a struggle for power between the sexes; this desire to "rule over" another is one result of human sin. But God's intention remains the same—equality in roles, authority, responsibility, and opportunities for service and ministry. So the rest of the Bible is seen as the story of redemption and restoration of all that was lost in the fall. In general, egalitarians tend to approach their conclusions holistically, interpreting passages that seem to restrict women in light of the flow of the whole Bible and redemptive history, and not as isolated texts that can be understood apart from this broader context.

A *complementarian* believes that women are gifted in many, many ways; that they are equal before God; but their function in a church is limited to the extent that they cannot have authority over men in such roles as elder or pastor.

Complementarians admit that females may have prophesied in the Scriptures, but they see prophecy as different than teaching or preaching. Complementarians build their case on the fact that the Bible never refers to female priests nor does Jesus include any females among his twelve disciples. (Egalitarians would respond that because Jesus only chose Jewish males for his twelve disciples obviously doesn't mean all disciples must be male and Jewish.)

Complementarians also cite as evidence for male leadership the two qualifications-for-elder passages—1 Timothy 3:1–6 and Titus 1:6–9 —which say that an elder should be "the husband of but one wife." (Egalitarians would respond that neither passage exclusively says that females should *not* be elders; the example of married male elders is merely the one given by Paul. Besides, if being married were a qualification, neither Paul nor Jesus himself would have qualified.)

Complementarians can structure their churches in ways that seek to fully honor and respect women while still limiting their functioning role within the church. Though complementarians disagree among themselves on what and how much a woman can legitimately do in church, some complementarian churches even allow women to teach men, however "under the authority" of the male elders. There is no biblical example for this practice, but it allows females to use their gifts with both sexes without violating complementarian beliefs.

Please do study further on this! What I've written here barely touches either argument. The point is, you should be able to explain whatever you personally believe or practice as a church. And don't avoid the crazy-sounding-at-first-glance passages; they are the ones that most likely you will be asked about!

Also, please watch your attitude toward Christians and churches with different beliefs than yours. As briefly illustrated here, there are good arguments for both positions.

SESSION 4:
IS THE CHURCH
HOMOPHOBIC?

GROUP STUDY AND DISCUSSION #2

3. Reflect on the following arguments (pages 60–65) and how you would explain each one. Here are interpretations from a conservative viewpoint:

The Sin of Sodom — Genesis 19

Historically, many Christians have used the story of Sodom to make a clear-cut case against homosexuality, citing the city's homosexual behavior as the sole reason for God's judgment. But it would be inaccurate to do so. The practice of homosexuality may have been one of the sins the city was judged for, but it was not the only sin. The primary focus in this account is the Sodomites' desire and intent to rape the visiting men — so rape (in this instance, homosexual rape) and violence appear to be two of the offending sins. A very similar story is recounted in Judges 19:22–30.

Ezekiel 16:49–50 also lists some of the sins of Sodom. There we read that the city was "arrogant, overfed and unconcerned; they did not help the poor and needy. They were haughty and did detestable things before me." Homosexuality is not specifically listed. Homosexuality may have indeed been among the "detestable things," and we can certainly conclude from Jude 7 ("Sodom and Gomorrah and the surrounding towns gave themselves up to sexual immorality and perversion") that their sins of a sexual nature greatly displeased God. But Sodom was most likely destroyed for several reasons, not just for the practice of homosexuality.

So there is truth in saying that the church has been one-sided in using the Sodom story to make a case for homosexuality as sin—when the sins of Sodom were many.

Leviticus Passages—Leviticus 18:22 and 20:13

The context here is God giving Israel laws to ensure that the people did not compromise and become like their pagan neighbors who worshiped other gods. Amid Leviticus 18's prohibitions against adultery, incest, sex during menstruation, and bestiality is this instruction in verse 22: "Do not have lie ["have sexual relations," TNIV] with a man as one lies with a woman; that is detestable." (The wording in Leviticus 20:13 is nearly the same.)

The word for "detestable" (*to'ebah*) does occur elsewhere in the Old Testament in relationship to the Canaanite fertility cults and ritual prostitution in pagan shrines and worship. However, the attempt to make a case based on these Leviticus passages that homosexuality is only to be considered morally wrong when associated with pagan worship rituals (and not in the case of consensual same-sex relationships) is not credible. If that were so, we would need to say the same for adultery, incest, and bestiality. But all of those behaviors are likewise condemned in the New Testament writings.

Critics also argue that those holding a conservative viewpoint arbitrarily pick and choose which Levitical laws *are* and *are not* sins today. If we choose to retain the passages that say homosexual relations are sin, why don't we also say that touching any dead pig skin (which would include a football) is sin (Lev. 11:7–8), or that wearing garments of two types of fabrics is sin (Lev. 19:19)?

This argument ties into a bigger question about the Mosaic Law—how much of it is still binding for us today? Critics are indeed correct when they contend that the Law (of which these verses are a part) is *not* totally binding for Christians today. We must look at the whole Bible to see which laws transcended Israel and carried through to New Testament teachings and which were specific to Israel and did not. For example, there were Old Testament dietary laws about what was "clean" and "unclean," such as the one about not touching dead pigs. But according to the New Testament (Acts 10), these things are now declared "clean." According to the Old Testament law, animal sacrifice was required, but Hebrews 12 says that we no longer need to sacrifice animals because Jesus was our sacrifice once and for all. The purpose for some of the Old Testament laws ended. But others carried through as moral laws that are to still be obeyed. For example, adultery is one of these moral laws — it's called sin in the Old Testament (Ex. 20:14) and sin in the New Testament (Matt. 19:9). And what about homosexuality? Read on.

"Natural" and "Unnatural" Sex — Romans 1:24–32

Some argue that the apostle Paul is *not* speaking here about natural homosexual sex, but about heterosexuals exchanging their normal heterosexuality to practice what would be "unnatural" sex for them. This is a weak argument. The late theologian Stanley Grenz wrote about this passage and argument in the book *Welcoming but Not Affirming: An Evangelical Response to Homosexuality* (Louisville, Ky.: Westminster John Knox, 1998). He states that Paul's wording in Romans 1:27 is very specific: "The verse does not speak of natural and unnatural feelings, but natural and unnatural function" (p. 49). It would be difficult to say this passage is talking about straight people who are "unnaturally" having homosexual sex. The contrast is between the physiological function of two people being "natural" with someone of the opposite sex and the "unnatural" nature of sexual activity with someone of the same sex. Jesus clarified what is natural in Matthew 19:4–6 when he spoke about a man and woman joining together as "one flesh."

Critics also argue that the passage is condemning homosexual sex as part of idolatrous worship, but not *all* homosexual sex. It is true that Paul is addressing idolatry here. But he lists a menu of sins which are a result of a fallen nature — among them gossip, envy, greed, and slander — not just homosexual sex. Just as we wouldn't say that gossip or slander is okay as long as it's not practiced as part of idolatrous worship, so also we can't say homosexual sex is okay as long as it is not practiced as part of idolatrous worship.

Again, I'm merely skimming the surface of this passage. Please refer to the session ending resources for books that provide a more detailed study.

Homosexual Prostitution Is the Sin, Not Homosexual Sex— 1 Corinthians 6:9–10; 1 Timothy 1:9–10

Let's start with 1 Timothy 1:9–10 (TNIV) which says:

> We also know that the law is made not for the righteous but for lawbreakers and rebels, the ungodly and sinful, the unholy and irreligious, for those who kill their fathers or mothers, for murderers, for the sexually immoral, for those practicing homosexuality [*arsenokoitai*], for slave traders and liars and perjurers.

Critics argue that most Christians have no idea that the Greek word used here is not the actual word "homosexual" but the word *arsenokoitai*. The meaning of *arsenokoitai* is unclear, they say, as it is a word Paul seems to have originated (which apparently is true).

However, that's not unusual; Paul coined a lot of words—over 150 in the New Testament. In this case, he created the word *arsenokoitai* by taking the popular Greek translation of the Old Testament, the Septuagint, and drawing two words from Leviticus 18:22 and Leviticus 20:13: "to lie (*koiten*) with a man (*arsenos*) as with a woman." Paul's connotation is evident—*arsenokoitai* describes two males being together sexually.

So even though the word *arsenokoitai* is uncommon, it is faithfully translated into English as "homosexual," based on its origins straight from Leviticus 18 and 20 talking about male homosexual sex.

Now let's look at 1 Corinthian 6:9–11 (TNIV):

> Or do you not know that wrongdoers will not inherit the kingdom of God? Do not be deceived: Neither the sexually immoral nor idolaters nor adulterers nor male prostitutes [*malokois*] nor practicing homosexuals [*arsenokotai*] nor thieves nor the greedy nor drunkards nor slanderers nor swindlers will inherit the kingdom of God. And that is what some of you were. But you were washed, you were sanctified, you were justified in the name of the Lord Jesus Christ and by the Spirit of our God.

In this passage the Greek word *malokois* proceeds *arsenokoitai*. *Malokois* means "soft" or "weak" and was often used by extrabiblical writers to refer to more passive, effeminate males or young males who sold themselves for sex. Thus, critics argue, 1 Corinthians 6:9 condemns effeminate male prostitutes and those paying for sex with them, not homosexuality in general.

There is indeed good reason for the word *malakois* to be translated as "male prostitute" here because it's likely that specific sin is one of those Paul is denouncing. But to say that the next word, *arsenokotai*, is referring specifically to those who pay for prostitutes and not practicing homosexuals in general is *not* accurate. The word as used in 1 Timothy does not seem to refer to men who pay for male prostitutes, nor does that seem to be the case here. The word likely means "homosexual" (practicing homosexuals), exactly as it has been translated.

Scot McKnight of North Park University is one theologian who has concluded that the passages we just looked at are specifically speaking about homosexual sex and not just homosexual prostitution or homosexual sex in idolatrous worship. He writes:

> One thing that can be said is that there is continuity between Genesis, Judges, Leviticus, and the early Christians on sexual purity and on strong denunciations of sexual perversions. There is no evidence that anyone addressed the distinction between same-sex orientation and same-sex sexual relations. What we do have, in my assessment, is that the Torah (in possible assumption, as I stated earlier) and the early Christians thought same-sex relations were unnatural ... I see no strong argument for concluding that the early Christians were thinking only either of pagan prostitution or pederasty; I think both may be involved, but those categories are only latently present in the Pauline texts. (Jesus Creed blog entry "Jesus and Homosexuality 5," http://www.jesuscreed.org/?p=755)

Jesus Did Not Talk about Homosexuality

Another argument becoming more common today is that because Jesus did not talk about homosexuality or address it is as a sin, he must not have felt it was too important or even a sin. It is true that Jesus was silent about homosexuality. But we need to remember that Jesus was silent about a lot of things. Because Jesus didn't mention something doesn't mean he didn't have an opinion about it. Jesus did not mention incest, and he would have had an opinion on that. It's difficult to make a case for an argument from silence. What we *do* have is the biblical account of what Jesus said about human sexuality. In Matthew 19:4–6, Jesus spoke of marriage and quoted the creation account of Adam and Eve's relationship (Genesis 2:23–24) to endorse heterosexual marriage and sex.

Beyond this strong statement of Jesus, the most compelling reason to hold to heterosexual marriage and sex as God's design is the story of the Bible as a whole. From the beginning, we see the beautiful story of man and woman being created different but complementary and making "one flesh." The one was not complete without the other. Only male and female together were capable of procreation and of fulfilling God's command to "be fruitful and multiply." Throughout the Bible we see again and again positive examples of marriages that are heterosexual; surely this is a strong indication of what God intended marriage to be.

The Problem—We Are All Sinners

To summarize this discussion, we must remember that we are all broken, fallen human beings who battle sins of various kinds. Though the evidence is inconclusive as to whether one is born with same-sex attraction, it develops through social and environmental influences, or a little of both, it is certainly an area of struggle for many men and women within the evangelical church, which teaches that homosexuality is a sin. Of course, those who do not hold to or know the Scriptures may not see the practice of homosexuality as a sin at all.

In our churches there are individuals with varying levels of same-sex attraction. Some are able to change and develop opposite-sex attraction. Some don't. We need to understand that there are those with same-sex attraction who love God tremendously, are faithful to the Scriptures, and have chosen to live celibate lives. Likely, most of these people are wondering if there is anyone in their church they can trust to talk with about this matter. How our churches talk about homosexuality, how we teach about it, and how we respond to all types of sin issues will make all the difference in determining if a person feels comfortable sharing their struggle. Are our churches safe, loving places for people to share their struggles not just with same-sex attraction but of all kinds?

Inside and outside our churches are people who are straight, gay, bisexual, and transgendered, all observing how the church talks about human sexuality—how we respond with our attitudes, our words, and our hearts. We may have a specific theological opinion about homosexuality, but how we express that opinion—how we love homosexual, bisexual, and transgendered people—will be in direct correlation to how we take Jesus' words when he said the second greatest command is to love our neighbors as ourselves (Matt. 22:34–40).

Ultimately, we must remember that God is powerful and his Spirit can change us. Recall Paul's words in 1 Corinthians 6 after he listed the kinds of sinners who would not inherit the kingdom of God: "And that is what some of you were. But you were washed, you were sanctified, you were justified in the name of the Lord Jesus Christ and by the Spirit of our God." When we put our faith in Jesus, we are washed, sanctified, and justified. Our struggles may not be eliminated, but we have hope, the power to resist temptation, and forgiveness when we fail.

SESSION 5: DO CHRISTIANS ARROGANTLY THINK ALL OTHER RELIGIONS ARE WRONG?

GROUP STUDY AND DISCUSSION #2

5. **Christians believe that Jesus is the one and only way to God. Can you list at least five Bible verses that back up that belief?**

   1) **John 14:6** — "I am the way and the truth and the life. No one comes to the Father except through me."

   2) **Acts 4:12 (TNIV)** — "Salvation is found in no one else, for there is no other name given under heaven by which we must be saved."

   3) **1 Timothy 2:5–6 (TNIV)** — "For there is one God and one mediator between God and human beings, Christ Jesus, himself human, who gave himself as a ransom for all people."

   4) **1 John 5:11–13 (TNIV)** — "And this is the testimony: God has given us eternal life and this life is in his Son. Whoever has the Son has life; whoever does not have the Son of God does not have life. I write these things to you who believe in the name of the Son of God so that you may know that you have eternal life."

   5) **1 Corinthians 8:6** — "Yet for us there is but one God, the Father, from whom all things came and for whom we live; and there is but one Lord, Jesus Christ, through whom all things came and through whom we live."

More visual rendering of the development of world faiths (mentioned on page 81).

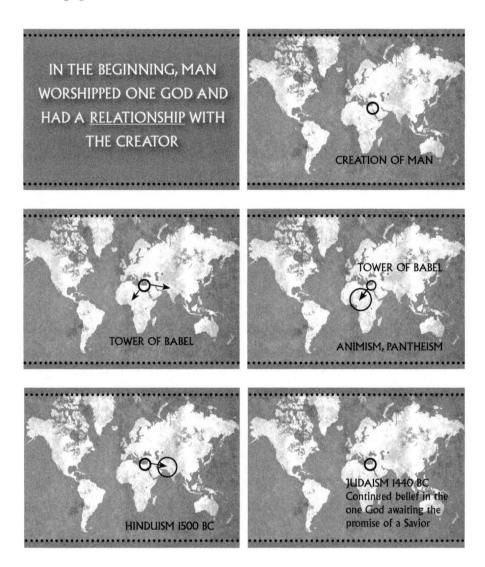

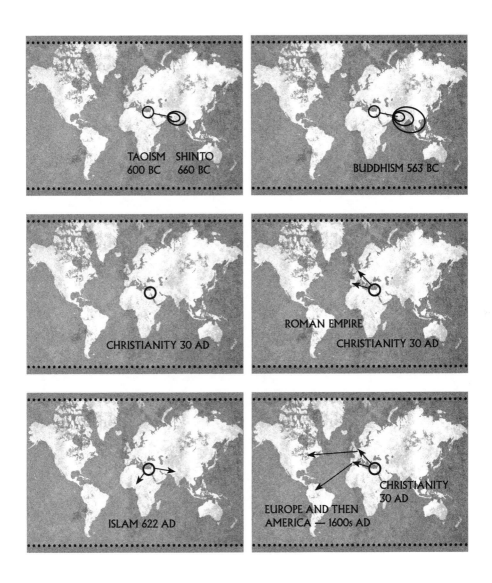

SESSION 6:
ARE CHRISTIANS FUNDAMENTALISTS WHO TAKE THE WHOLE BIBLE LITERALLY?

GROUP STUDY AND DISCUSSION #1

6. Pagan religions that predate Christianity have stories of the killing of a god and his resurrection, a virgin birth, having twelve followers, and so on, and Christianity merely included these pagan elements to deify Jesus. What would you say to Dustan who has read these very claims in books by respected university professors and historical scholars?

Claims that Christianity borrowed from pagan religions to deify Jesus sound quite convincing and may alarm the uninformed. Similar stories throughout history do include a "god" who has a child through a human mother and a dying savior who rises from the dead. And it's true that the date of our Christmas, December 25, was the birthday for pagan gods throughout time—Attis, Mithras, Dionysus, and Osiris.

But when you research these claims in depth, you will find that the similarities are far more superficial than substantial. Yes, there are definitely patterns throughout history—but ultimately the patterns when examined closely demonstrate that people must stretch and read into them to make them fit the biblical story.

December 25 is the winter solstice, and many pagan religions throughout time did state their "god" was born on that day. However, the Bible does not say when Jesus was born. December 25 was a date selected by the early Catholic church in an attempt to overshadow the other celebrations, not to try to deify Jesus.

The point here is to realize that it is more and more common to hear that Christianity is not unique but simply borrowed from pagan religions. Don't be surprised by the claim but instead have confidence that there are plausible answers to the challenge. See the recommended resources at the end of the session for further help.

GROUP STUDY AND DISCUSSION #2

1. **List at least three verses from the Bible that claim God inspired it in its entirety.**

   1) **2 Peter 1:20–21 (TNIV)** — "No prophecy of Scripture came about by the prophet's own interpretation of things. For prophecy never had its origin in the human will, but prophets, though human, spoke from God as they were carried along by the Holy Spirit."

   2) **2 Timothy 3:16–17 (TNIV)** — "All Scripture is God-breathed and is useful for teaching, rebuking, correcting and training in righteousness, so that all God's people may be thoroughly equipped for every good work."

   3) **Matthew 5:18–19** — "I tell you the truth, until heaven and earth disappear, not the smallest letter, not the least stroke of a pen, will by any means disappear from the Law until everything is accomplished. Anyone who breaks one of the least of these commandments and teaches others to do the same will be called least in the kingdom of heaven, but whoever practices and teaches these commands will be called great in the kingdom of heaven."

2. **List five solid reasons why you have confidence that the Bible is inspired and trustworthy.**

   Below is a quick list, but you will need to do more research for further explanation.

APPENDIX

SESSION 6: ARE CHRISTIANS FUNDAMENTALISTS
WHO TAKE THE WHOLE BIBLE LITERALLY?

1) **The preservation of the Bible throughout time.** Yes, errors have crept in through time. But there is an amazing accuracy of preservation through time that exceeds other ancient documents.

2) **The unity of the Bible.** The Bible was written by more than forty different authors over a period of fifteen hundred years in three different languages. Writers ranged from a doctor (Luke) to a fisherman (Peter) to a lawyer (Matthew). Yet despite the diversity, there is a great unity and unifying message.

3) **The evidence from archaeology.** The Bible contains numerous references to history, geographical places, and the like, so the odds are high that if it were not inspired, there would be a lot of errors. But the Bible proves to be an accurate record of various cities, sites, and stories throughout history that are backed up by archaeological evidence.

4) **Fulfilled prophecy.** Yes, there is a lot of biblical prophecy yet to be fulfilled. But you can point to Jesus' prediction of the destruction of the temple in Jerusalem (Matt. 24:1–2), which came to pass in AD 70. Many Old Testament prophecies of the coming Messiah were fulfilled in Jesus (see Isa. 53, for example). And Isaiah 11:11–12 predicted that the Jews would one day return to the land of Israel, which occurred in 1948 when Israel was formally reborn. Fulfilled prophecy backs up the claim that the Bible is inspired.

5) **Changed lives.** The Bible does change lives (Heb. 4:12). Not only can you point to accounts of transformation within the Bible itself, but you can also share how God has used the Scriptures to change your own life.

3. **Can you list some of the reasons you believe that the compiled books of the Bible are the ones that God wanted and that the ones left out were under dispute?**

People did not arbitrarily pick and choose which books of the Bible were inspired or not; they *recognized* which books were inspired by God and included them in the canon. *Canon* is simply the Greek word for "a straight rod" or "a carpenter's rule." Thus the term became known for books that were divinely inspired and part of the Bible.

As the Old Testament (Hebrew Bible) was written, it was compiled and kept by the religious leaders of Israel. The Torah (first five books of the Hebrew Bible) were probably accepted as inspired shortly after they were written. Moses had the books of the Law placed in the ark of the covenant, where they were kept during the wilderness journey as well as once the permanent temple in Jerusalem was built (Deut. 31:9, 26; Josh. 24:26; 1 Sam. 10:25; 2 Kings 22:8).

As the historical and prophetic books were written, they were gathered and placed in the temple. By around 167 BC, the current Old Testament books as we know them had all been written. Jesus spoke of their format much like we have today—the Law, the prophets, and the Psalms (Luke 24:44). A more complete recognition of the current Hebrew canon occurred around 90 AD by Jewish scholars at the Council of Jamnia. By AD 250 there was nearly universal agreement on the canon of Hebrew Scripture.

The process of recognizing and collecting the New Testament began in the early days of the church. We read that even while the New Testament was being written, some of the books were being recognized as inspired and as Scripture. Peter recognized Paul's writings as Scripture (2 Peter 3:15–16). Some of the books of the New Testament were being circulated among the churches (Col. 4:16; 1 Thess. 5:27).

In the post-apostolic age, the New Testament as we know it today continued to be shaped. In AD 95, Clement of Rome mentioned at least eight New Testament books. In AD 115, Ignatius of Antioch acknowledged seven books. Polycarp, a disciple of the apostle John, acknowledged fifteen books in AD 108. In AD 185, Irenaeus mentioned twenty-one books. Hippolytus recognized twenty-two books during his lifetime (AD 170–235). The New Testament books subject to the most controversy and debate were Hebrews, James, 2 Peter, 2 John, and 3 John, but they were eventually recognized.

The first canon, the Muratorian Canon compiled in AD 170, included all of the present New Testament books except Hebrews,

James, and 3 John. In the early 200s, Origen listed all twenty-seven New Testament books, but indicated six were still being questioned. The Council of Laodicea in AD 363 stated that only the Old Testament (along with the Apocrypha) and the twenty-seven books of the New Testament were to be read in the churches. A letter of Athanasius in AD 367 formally named all twenty-seven books as the New Testament. The Council of Hippo in AD 393 affirmed the same twenty-seven books as inspired and authoritative. The final determination of the canon occurred at the Council of Carthage in AD 397.

Although there weren't any written "here's how you recognize that a book is inspired" rules, the councils that met to discuss canonization followed some basic tests and questions such as:

- Was the author an apostle or have a close connection with an apostle?
- Is the book being accepted by the church at large?
- Did the book contain consistency of doctrine and orthodox teaching?
- Did the book bear evidence of high moral and spiritual value for believers?

Again, it is critical to remember that it was not the church that determined the canon, but God. It was simply a matter of God moving the church to realize what he had already decided upon. He oversaw the process to ensure that the selection was unaffected by human error.

Knowing the origin of the Bible, or canonization process, ought to be one of the most important things that we learn because it is from the Bible that all our doctrines and beliefs come. We should be able to articulate where the Bible came from and why we trust it.

5. **In the space below provide a quick definition of each term in relation to the Bible and, in the case of the final five, an example from Scripture.**

Literal = The words used mean exactly what they say. Much of the Bible is meant to be read literally, but just like most literature, the Bible also includes other genres which must be understood as such for proper interpretation. Some of the most theologically important words of the Bible are figures of speech that are not meant to be read or interpreted literally.

Figurative = Figurative language includes metaphor, simile, hyperbole, and anthropomorphism (see definitions that follow). Jesus often explained his ministry in figurative language rather than in plain words.

Metaphor = A metaphor is an implied comparison that does not use the words *like* or *as*. In John 15:1 Jesus states, "I am the true vine." This does not mean he is a literal vine, but that he can be compared to one.

Simile = An explicit comparison that uses the words *like* or *as*. Many parables of Jesus use similes, as they often begin with the phrase "the kingdom of God is like ...." You see examples of similes in Mark 1:10 and Luke 13:34.

Hyperbole = Hyperbole is a grossly exaggerated description or statement made to emphasize a point. For example, in Matthew 7:3–5 Jesus talks about taking a plank out of one's eye. Other examples are Deuteronomy 1:28; Matthew 5:29–30, 16:26; and Acts 27:34.

Anthropomorphism = Language that speaks of God in human terms, ascribing to him human characteristics or emotions. For example, 1 Peter 3:12 refers to the Lord's eyes, ears, and face. Other examples are Exodus 8:19 and Psalm 91:4.

Apocalyptic = Parts of the Bible that specifically use poetry and strong images that would be familiar to the original readers, usually about future events. Apocalyptic language uses symbols and numbers to communicate meaning. Parts of the book of Daniel are apocalyptic as well as the book of Revelation.

Understanding these different genres is important for Bible interpretation. Knowing who wrote the book, when it was written, and what was happening in the culture at the time it was written also have major implications for how we understand a passage's meaning. See the recommended resources for some basic Bible study methods materials.

And remember that it is more than skills that help us understand the Scriptures. We can never forget the Spirit of God's role in the process (1 Cor. 2:11–13). We also must admit that we are fallible, sinful human beings, which is why we have differences when it comes to interpretations about issues such as the role of women in ministry or the end times. Our attitude should always be humble toward and respectful of other evangelical Christians who have different views.

6. List the original "five fundamentals" of the Christian faith.

1) The inspiration (and inerrancy) of the Scriptures

2) The divinity of Jesus

3) The virgin birth of Jesus

4) Substitionary atonement by Jesus

5) The bodily resurrection and future return of Jesus

Do You Like Jesus but Not the Church?

Exploring Uncomfortable Questions about Christianity and the Church

Dan Kimball

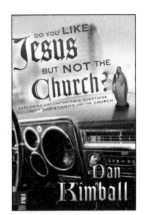

(A Book for Anyone Seeking Answers to These Questions)

Ask someone today what they think of Jesus and chances are you'll get a positive response. Ask their opinion of Christians and the church and the reply will probably be less favorable. Why? As our culture has changed, negative perceptions of the Christianity and church have multiplied. Skeptics deserve thoughtful and humble responses to questions such as:

- Would Jesus even attend a church today?
- Are Christians homophobic?
- Are Christians fundamentalists who take the entire Bible literally?
- Are Christians closed-minded and judgmental?
- Do Christians arrogantly think that all other religions are wrong?
- Is the church a place that oppresses females?

Whether someone needs help responding to these questions or perhaps has these questions themselves, *Do You Like Jesus but Not the Church?* will provide hope and guidance.

For more information, go to *www.theylikejesus.com*.

Softcover 978-0-310-25418-8

Pick up a copy today at your favorite bookstore!

ZONDERVAN®
.com

They Like Jesus but Not the Church

Insights from Emerging Generations

Dan Kimball

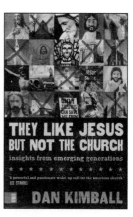

(A Book for Church Leaders)

Many people today, especially among emerging generations, are not resonating with church or organized Christianity. Some are leaving the church and others were never part of the church in the first place. Yet they are still interested in Jesus. This ministry resource book for church leaders explores some of the reasons emerging generations are leaving the church or not coming at all, drawn straight from conversations with some twenty- and thirty-somethings. It tackles perceptions such as:

- The church is judgmental and closed-minded.
- The church is organized religion with a political agenda.
- The church is homophobic.
- The church oppresses women.
- The church arrogantly thinks all other religions are wrong.
- The church is made up of "fundamentalists" who take the whole Bible literally.

Besides exploring these negative perceptions, each chapter offers ways for church leaders to biblically respond, then ends with discussion questions as well as resource listings. The book also gives examples of churches who are holding to truth and yet seeing emerging generations connect or reconnect with a church community.

Softcover 978-0-310-24590-2

Pick up a copy today at your favorite bookstore!

The Emerging Church

Vintage Christianity for New Generations

Dan Kimball

Includes
- Samples and photos of emerging church worship gatherings
- Recommended resources for the emerging church

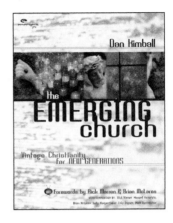

The seeker-sensitive movement revolutionized the way we did church and introduced countless baby boomers to Jesus. Yet trends show that today's post-Christian generations are not responding like the generations before them. As we enter a new cultural era, what do worship services look like that are connecting with the hearts of emerging generations? How do preaching, leadership, evangelism, spiritual formation, and, most of all, how we even think of "church" need to change?

The Emerging Church goes beyond just theory and gets into very practical ways of assisting you in your local church circumstances. There is no one right way, no model for us all to emulate. But there is something better. Dan Kimball calls it "Vintage Christianity": a refreshing return to an unapologetically sacred, raw, historical, and Jesus-focused missional ministry. Vintage Christianity connects with emerging post-seeker generations who are very open spiritually but are not interested in church.

For pastors, leaders, and every concerned Christian, Kimball offers a riveting and easy-to-grasp exploration of today's changing culture and gives insight into the new kind of churches that are emerging in its midst. Included is running commentary by Rick Warren, Brian McLaren, Howard Hendricks, and others.

Softcover 978-0-310-24564-3

Pick up a copy today at your favorite bookstore!

Emerging Worship

Creating Worship Gatherings for New Generations

Dan Kimball

Churches are aging. Even among mega-churches with their modern technology and huge number of members, whole generations are now missing. In order to reach the 18–35 year olds, churches need to incorporate alternative worship services into their ministries that meet the unique needs of the emerging generations.

In a conversational, narrative style, author Dan Kimball guides church leaders on how to create alternative services from start to finish. Using anecdotes from his own experience at Graceland, Kimball presents six creative models, providing real-life examples of each type. *Emerging Worship* covers key topics including

- Developing a prayer team
- Evaluating the local mission field and context
- Determining leaders and a vision-based team
- Understanding why youth pastors are usually the ideal staff to start a new service
- Recognizing the difference in values between emerging worship and the rest of the church
- Asking critical questions beforehand

Softcover 978-0-310-25644-1

Pick up a copy today at your favorite bookstore!

ZONDERVAN®
.com

We want to hear from you. Please send your comments about this book to us in care of zreview@zondervan.com. Thank you.

ZONDERVAN.com/
AUTHORTRACKER
follow your favorite authors